D0820412

Confederate Shipbuilding

Confederate Shipbuilding

William N. Still, Jr.
University of South Carolina Press

Published in Columbia, South Carolina, by the
University of South Carolina Press

Manufactured in the United States of America

07   06   05   04   03   6   5   4   3   2

Library of Congress Cataloging-in-Publication Data

Still, William N.
    Confederate shipbuilding.

    Originally published: Athens : University of
Georgia Press, 1969.
    Bibliography: p.
    Includes index.
    1. Shipbuilding industry—Confederate States
of America. I. Title.
VM299.6.S75 1987   338.4'762382'00975   86-30829
ISBN 0-87249-511-6

Contents

Acknowledgments

I AM INDEBTED to many individuals and institutions for aid in the preparation of this manuscript. I wish especially to express my appreciation to Professor Robert E. Johnson of the University of Alabama for his encouragement and help, to my former colleagues at Mississippi State College for Women, Dr. Thomas H. Baker and Dr. May Ringold, for reading the manuscript and making valuable suggestions, to Mr. William E. Geoghegan, Museum Specialist, Division of Transportation, Smithsonian Institute, for his examination and criticism of Chapter I, and to Dr. Charles Price of East Carolina University for his advice, particularly on Chapter III. Much of the research was done through the generous financial assistance of Mississippi State College for Women. East Carolina University provided me with assistance for typing. My wife, Mildred, accompanied me on many research trips and aided me in innumerable ways in completing the work. Without her endeavor, encouragement, and understanding this volume would not have been possible.

For this second edition, I am particularly grateful to Robert Holcome, Director of the Confederate Naval Museum, Columbus, Georgia. Bob's careful reading of the first edition resulted in several changes in the text as well as the elimination of errors. In addition, he generously provided new illustrations.

William N. Still, Jr.

East Carolina University
Greenville, North Carolina

Preface

DESPITE the vast amount of literature written about the American Civil War there are still topics that have not been adequately examined. Among these is the subject of this monograph. The importance of naval power in the outcome of the Civil War is generally recognized by historians. The Union blockade, amphibious operations along the Southern coastline, and operations of the Federal fresh-water navy on the Mississippi River and its tributaries were contributing factors in the final defeat of the Confederacy. Historians are also aware that Southerners tried to build a navy to combat the Northern fleets, but the traditional view held by Bern Anderson, E. Merton Coulter, Joseph T. Durkin, James G. Randall, and Frank Vandiver among others is that they met with indifferent success, primarily because they were "without the means of constructing one." The South, as Durkin has observed in his *Stephen R. Mallory: Confederate Navy Chief*, "had neither shipyards (save Norfolk, which was soon lost, and Pensacola, which was inadequate and also, finally, captured) nor workshops, steam mills or foundries, except on the most limited scale. . . . There was not, in the whole Confederacy, the means of turning out a complete steam engine of a size suitable for ships. . . . There was not a rolling mill capable of turning out two-and-a-half inch plate. There was not sufficient force of skilled mechanics."

While working on a study of Confederate armored vessels, I came to suspect that the dismal picture painted by Durkin and others was not quite accurate. For one thing Southerners did build and place in operation about half of the ironclads laid down. Although these vessels were not as sophisticated as those built by Northerners, they proved to be successful men-of-war.

Confederate Shipbuilding is an exploration of the efforts by Southerners to build warships. I have not attempted to outline in detail the chronology of naval building in the Confederacy. Rather, a topical approach has been chosen with emphasis on the major problems that were encountered. The first chapter does survey briefly the shipbuilding program from 1861 through 1865; after that in order are chapters on facilities, materials, and labor. Three questions are examined and, I hope are answered: Did the Confederates have the potential to build warships? How successful were they in building warships? What factors were most responsible for their failure?

Many of the Confederacy's serious weaknesses such as inadequate industrial, financial, and transportation facilities; state rights; and internal dissension are illustrated in this study. For that reason an examination of the shipbuilding program should contribute to our understanding of the Confederacy's collapse.

Introduction

AS MANY WRITERS have emphasized, the conflict between the North and South was an industrial war, and economic factors played an important role in determining its outcome. Northern superiority in industrial resources as well as manpower was nearly overwhelming. Of the 31,443,321 inhabitants of the United States in 1860, the eleven states forming the Confederacy embraced approximately nine million, of whom over three and a half million were slaves. According to the 1860 census there were approximately 1,300,000 industrial workers in the North compared to 110,000 in the South. The twenty-three states that remained in the Union manufactured more than nine-tenths of the industrial goods produced in the United States. At the outbreak of war the North produced annually, according to value, seventeen times as much cotton and woolen goods as did the South; thirty times as many boots and shoes; twenty times as much pig iron; thirteen times as much bar, sheet, and railroad iron; twenty-four times as many locomotive engines; more than 500 times as much general hardware; seventeen times as much agricultural machinery; thirty-two times as many firearms; and five times as much tonnage in ships and boats. The eleven states that comprised the Confederacy also lacked other branches of manufacturing important to an independent industrial system. The section manufactured no steel, no car wheels, and no sewing machines. Even more significantly she possessed none of the "parent industries"—the machine tools that produced the machinery to turn out the implements of war.[1]

If, then, the Union had an overwhelming preponderance in most sources of economic power was the defeat of the Confederacy inevitable? Probably not, for as many historians of the war have pointed out, the Confederacy did not have to win in order to win, but had only to convince the North that coercion was impossible or too costly. The grand strategy or policy of the North was to restore the Union, and in order to accomplish this objective she had to conquer the South—to invade and hold an area as great as all western Europe except Italy and Scandinavia. The Confederacy could afford to lose all the battles and campaigns and still win, if she could persuade the North that the price of victory was too high.

The general military policy of the Confederacy was defensive. This was in part an inevitable response to Northern strategy and in part due to the nature of the war. She was not trying to conquer the North, but wanted only to preserve her recently-proclaimed independence. For that reason Confederate strategy generally developed around the same objectives toward which the Union forces were aiming. In practice this meant an attempt to post adequate forces at all threatened points along the extensive frontier of the Confederacy, including the western rivers and seacoast. This policy dispersed Confederate resources, inferior to those of the North, over a wide strategic circumference and yielded the strategic initiative to the enemy.

This strategy of defense determined Confederate naval policy. The blockade followed by the implementation of General Winfield Scott's plan to recover the South (a plan which envisioned the seizure of Southern ports to seal off all commerce and the control of the main transportation arteries from Ohio to the Gulf of Mexico) made inescapable the navy's concentrated efforts to defend the key ports, inlets, bays, and rivers in the beleaguered nation. As part of this strategy, cruisers such as the *Alabama, Nashville,* and *Shenandoah* were to attack and destroy Union shipping in order to divert naval vessels from the blockade. The Confederate navy made no serious effort to challenge Union naval superiority at sea. Its primary objectives were simply to prevent the capture of key points within the Confederacy and to hold or re-open the major ports to foreign commerce. In order to accomplish these objectives, the Confederate government had to create a navy.

Confederate Shipbuilding

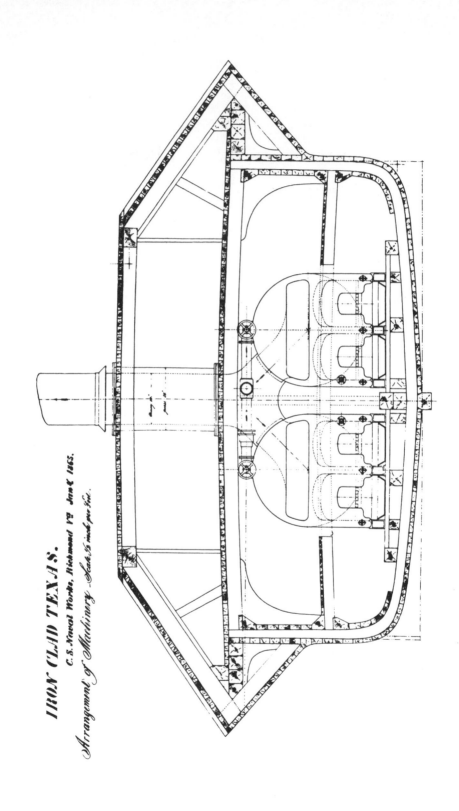

IRON CLAD TEXAS.

C. S. Naval Works, Richmond Va. June 1865.

Arrangement of Machinery. Scale ¼ inch per foot.

The Program

UPON a rainy afternoon in February 1862, the city of Mobile, Alabama, found itself the scene of an event that is not uncommon in a seaport—the launching of a ship. Despite the inclement weather an unusually large number of people, including women and children, turned out to witness the event, for the vessel to be commissioned the *Morgan* was the first warship to be built in that city and the first to be built from the keel up in the Confederate States of America. Only twelve months before, delegates from six Southern states had met in Montgomery, Alabama, 178 miles north of Mobile, to organize a government.

On February 21, 1861, the Confederate Congress created a navy department, and shortly afterwards Stephen R. Mallory assumed his duties as secretary of the department. Mallory was perhaps as well qualified as most appointees to cabinet positions —the essential prerequisite being a certain amount of administrative ability. He certainly had that as well as a limited knowledge of naval affairs acquired from commanding a longboat in the Seminole War, from his work as collector of customs, from his experience as an admiralty lawyer in Key West, and from serving as the chairman of the Naval

Affairs Committee while a United States senator from Florida. In the latter position he developed an interest in ship design, naval ordnance, and other technological subjects that served him well when he became Confederate secretary of the navy.[1]

Mallory was able to exercise much more direct control over the navy than the various secretaries of war ever exerted over the army. Jefferson Davis, Confederate president, had little interest in or understanding of naval power. Whether because of his absorbing concern with land warfare or some other reason, his published and unpublished correspondence contains few references to naval matters. Mallory's unpublished diary, so revealing on presidential political and social matters, has little to say about this. When he does mention Davis and the navy it usually reflects the President's negative attitude. For example, Mallory's struggle with the War Department over workmen led him to write: "The President [refuses] . . . to permit a man to leave the army to work on gunboats." Coordination between the two services is essential in any war, and especially so in the type of conflict fought between the North and South. Coordination, however, was not present on the cabinet level between the secretaries of navy and war, and more frequently than not it was absent on lower levels. Davis could have smoothed out many of the difficulties by assuming a more positive role, but he usually referred most matters to the two secretaries to be worked out.[2] Mallory did retain the president's confidence throughout the war, an impressive example of loyalty considering the many reversals suffered by the navy.

Mallory was also greatly handicapped because the president's cabinet, Congress, and the public considered the army to be more important in the Confederate war effort; the navy's role was secondary. The naval secretary struggled continually for his department's share of money, manpower, transportation, manufacturing facilities, and essential materials.

The opposition of many of the state governors to the central government's war policies inevitably affected the navy. In the spring and summer of 1861 there was some trouble over the transfer of state navies to the Confederate government. Later Mallory became involved in controversies with several governors, particularly Joseph Brown of Georgia and Zebulon Vance of North Carolina, over transportation facilities, conscription, and iron.

Mallory has generally been lauded by historians for what Durkin called "a kind of impulsive progressivism, which, although it sometimes led him astray, enabled him in other instances to recognize and to develop with boldness sound new principles."[3] Among these "new principles" and probably his chief claim to fame was the ironclad. There can be no question about his emphasis on ironclad construction throughout the war. But a number of individuals, including several naval officers, had encouraged him to purchase or build armored vessels even before his decision to do so. John P. Jones recorded in his diary in May 1861, "I have heard [Mallory] . . . soundly abused for not accepting some propositions . . . to build ironclad steam rams."[4] Mallory was also cool toward a torpedo boat developed by an army officer, but later he approved the construction of a number of smaller torpedo boats.

There was no chief of naval operations or its equivalent in the Confederate States navy for Mallory to consult on technical, tactical, and strategic matters. The naval secretary, however, relied heavily upon a number of naval officers for advice. Commanding officers of squadrons and vessels acting independently were given considerable discretion concerning tactical operations. Mallory occasionally sent out suggestions for action, but seldom did he order a particular move. This was particularly true of the coastal defense units and those operating on inland waters. On the other hand he held a tight reign over naval shipbuilding and related activities. He frequently sent naval officers to examine vessels under construction and report on their progress.

When Norfolk, Pensacola, Memphis, and New Orleans were lost in the spring of 1862, the navy bore the brunt of public censure. The fact that the army was as much to blame for these disasters as the navy was completely ignored. When Mallory came under attack on the floor of Congress, he demanded an investigation of his department. The investigation was subsequently held, and after several hundred pages of testimony was taken the department was fully exonerated.

Mallory's performance as wartime secretary was impressive, particularly when his task is compared to that of Union naval secretary Gideon Welles. The United States began the Civil War woefully unprepared with 7,600 men and ninety warships, of which forty-two were actually in commission; whereas the Confederacy had virtually no navy at all. In addition the North had a large merchant marine to draw seamen and ships from, as well as extensive shipyards and machinery fabricating facilities. Eight of the ten navy yards were also in the Union. Yet the South was able to build a navy, and although small in comparison to the one created by the North it was nonetheless respectable. Mallory deserves a large share of the credit for this.

When the newly-appointed secretary arrived in Montgomery to take over his post, he found that his most immediate concern was organizing the department and finding assignments for more than two-hundred former United States naval officers who had resigned their commissions or who would do so in the next few weeks. The supply of commissioned officers was out of proportion to the demand, since the Confederate government possessed only ten small vessels. While Mallory recognized the necessity of creating a respectable navy, Congress at that time was interested only in establishing a small naval auxiliary force to cooperate with the army.

Of the ninety ships in the United States Navy at the time of President Abraham Lincoln's inauguration, only one, the *Fulton*, an old side-wheeler built in 1837 and laid up at the Pensacola Navy Yard, was seized by Southerners. Naval officers from Southern states in command of United States vessels refused to turn their vessels over to Confederate authorities. John Newton Maffitt, commanding the screw steamer *Crusader* in Mobile Bay, was ordered to surrender her to the state of Alabama. He replied, "I may be overpowered, . . . but, in that event, what will be left of the *Crusader* will not be worth taking."[5]

In addition to the *Fulton* the Confederacy acquired by purchase or capture, four revenue cutters, three slavers, and two small privately-owned coastal steamers. These ten vessels, carrying a total of fifteen guns, formed the nucleus of the Confederate States navy when it was organized in February 1861.[6] The incorporation of various state navies added additional vessels. Georgia and South Carolina each supplied two small gunboats, and after secession both Virginia and North Carolina transferred five ships to Confederate service.[7]

The firing on Fort Sumter, April 12, 1861, followed in rapid order by Lincoln's call to the state governors for 75,000 troops, his proclamation of a blockade of Southern ports from South Carolina to Texas, and the secession of Virginia, North Carolina, Tennessee, and Arkansas, made it essential for the Confederate government to obtain additional warships immediately.

The conversion of purchased merchant steamers into warships was an obvious way of strengthening the naval force, but Mallory's efforts in this direction were not particularly successful. He attempted fruitlessly to obtain vessels in Canada and the United States. In March a commission of three officers went to New Orleans to examine vessels there and to report whether or not there were any suitable for warships. Although the report was not encouraging, the navy purchased the *Habana* and the *Marquis de la Habana*, commissioned as the *Sumter* and *McRae* in the Confederate navy. By the middle of July three additional vessels, the *Jackson* at New Orleans, and the *Sampson* and *Resolute* at Savannah, all tugboats, were operating as coastal defense gunboats. Mallory was also negotiating the purchase of the steamer *Florida* in Mobile and two small steamers on Lake Pontchartrain.

To the naval secretary, the conversion of river and ocean steamers into gunboats was a stop-gap measure. He recognized the weakness of these vessels as warships, particularly the paddle-wheel steamers. A few days after Fort Sumter fell to the Confederacy, he wrote Jefferson Davis: "Side-wheel steamers, from the exposure of their machinery to shot and shell, and their liability to be disabled by a single shot, from the fact that if prevented from steering they are helpless as sailers; and that they can not carry to sea sufficient coal for any but short cruises, are regarded as unfit for cruising men of war."[8] Mallory added in his report to the Confederate president that he hoped to purchase "cruisers" abroad. In fact, it was apparent to the naval secretary that his best source for the immediate acquisition of warships was in Europe. In May James D. Bulloch and James H. North were sent to England on a buying mission. A number of fast commerce raiders, of which the most famous were the *Alabama* and *Shenandoah*, were purchased and proceeded along with their tenders to play havoc with Union shipping. Contracts were also let with companies in England and France for armored vessels.

Mallory was convinced that the Southern states could not achieve parity with the North in numbers of ships; but inequality of numbers might be compensated for by invulnerability. Hence his decision to acquire ironclads. On May 10 the naval secretary wrote to the chairman of the Confederate House Committee on Naval Affairs:

> I regard the possession of an iron-armored ship as a matter of the first necessity. Such a vessel at this time could traverse the entire coast of the United States, prevent all blockades, and encounter, with a fair prospect of success, their entire Navy. If to cope with them upon the sea we follow their example and build wooden ships, we shall have to construct several at one time; for one or two ships would fall an easy prey to her comparatively numerous steam frigates. But inequality of numbers may be compensated by invulnerability; and thus not only does economy but naval success dictate the wisdom and expediency of fighting with iron against wood. . . .

This letter ended with a recommendation that funds be appropriated to purchase ironclad vessels in Europe. That same day Congress allotted $2,000,000 for this purpose. Only one of the ironclads contracted for in Europe, the *Stonewall* built in France, came into the possession of the Confederacy, and she accomplished nothing before the war ended.

During the spring of 1861 Mallory showed little interest in constructing warships within the Confederacy, preferring to concentrate on purchasing and converting steamers into gunboats and procuring vessels in Europe. In March Congress had appropriated $1,000,000 and in May an additional $2,000,000 for the purchase or construction of warships, but most of it was to be expended in Europe. A contract with John Hughes and Company of New Orleans on June 28 for the completion of a frame already on the stocks as a gunboat was the only contract made until Congress appropriated additional funds in August 1861.[10]

While Mallory was developing his naval building program, Union Secretary of the Navy Welles was trying to get the blockade established. On May 9 Captain W. W. McKean arrived off Charleston in the *Niagara*. Three days later the *Water Witch* arrived off Pensacola with Lincoln's proclamation, and Captain H. A. Adams, senior naval officer in the Gulf of Mexico, sent official notice of it ashore to Confederate General Braxton Bragg. By the middle of July Flag Officer S. H. Stringham, in command of the Atlantic Blockading Squadron, had eleven ships stationed off Savannah, Charleston, and the North Carolina coast, with additional vessels watching the mouths of the James, Rappahannock, and York Rivers in Virginia, while Flag Officer William Mervine, in command of the Gulf squadron, had blockaders cruising off Mobile, the Mississippi deltas, and Galveston, Texas.

Union strategy, which included regaining control of the Mississippi River, resulted in the decision to build gunboats in the West. By the middle of August three steamers had been converted into gunboats and others were under construction. While the army under General Irvin McDowell was recovering from the debacle of Bull Run, other Northern forces, naval and land, were beginning to cooperate in operations that would ultimately give the Union important bases along the coast of the Confederacy and control of the entire Mississippi valley.

In the late summer and early fall of 1861 the Union army and navy began a series of amphibious operations along the southern coastline. On August 28-29 Forts Clark and Hatteras on the North Carolina coast yielded to troops under the command of the politician-general, Benjamin Butler; and on

November 7 Union forces gained control of Port Royal, South Carolina, in a brief but important engagement. At the same time reports of gunboat construction and other activities in cities along the upper Mississippi and Ohio Rivers alarmed governments in the Confederate states adjacent to the lower Mississippi. These operations increased public pressure on governmental officials, both Confederate and state, to strengthen coastal defenses. From state legislatures and the Confederate Congress came demands that gunboats for river and harbor defense be constructed as rapidly as possible. This determined Mallory to initiate naval construction within the Confederacy.

His resolution to acquire armored warships prompted him to investigate the possibility of constructing an ironclad steamer in the Confederacy. Naval officers in various states were ordered to ascertain whether or not wrought iron plates "of any given thickness from two and one-half to five inches" could be manufactured by local foundries or iron works. Their replies were negative. The few iron works in the Confederacy were already under contract with the government and were quite reluctant to undertake expensive conversion of machinery in order to roll heavy iron plate. The one exception to this was Tredegar Iron Works in Richmond which did have the facilities to roll one to two-inch plate.[11] Shortly after the capital of the Confederacy was transferred from Montgomery to Richmond, Mallory ordered Lieutenant John M. Brooke to prepare plans for an armored warship. Brooke, who was not a draftsman but an ordnance expert, provided the drawings, which the naval secretary approved and turned over to naval constructor John L. Porter to be drawn up in detail. Later at the suggestion of Brooke and a naval engineer, the secretary ordered the application of Brooke's design to the recently raised frigate *Merrimack*. Conversion of the *Merrimack* into the ironclad *Virginia* started in July.

Four additional armored vessels were authorized for construction by the Confederate government in 1861. On July 30 Mallory conferred with a group of his officers about the possibility of creating a fleet of ironclads on western rivers capable of opposing an invasion and, if necessary, going to sea. Shortly thereafter, John T. Shirley, a prominent Memphis constructor who was concerned over river defenses, proposed to build ironclad gunboats for river service. The proposal was carried to the Confederate House of Representatives by David M. Currin, a member of the House Naval Affairs Committee from Memphis. In August a naval appropriations bill was passed which included $160,000 "for the construction, equipment, and armament of two ironclad gunboats, for the defense of the Mississippi River and the city of Memphis." Shortly afterwards Shirley laid down the keels of the two vessels to be named the *Arkansas* and *Tennessee*.[12]

The bill which provided for ironclads to be constructed at Memphis also included an appropriation of $800,000 "for floating defenses of New Orleans." Two days after Davis signed the bill, two brothers, Asa and Nelson Tift, arrived in Richmond and conferred with Mallory. Although the Tifts had no experience in shipbuilding—Nelson was a Georgia planter, and Asa had been an editor, merchant, president of a railroad, legislator, and owner of a boat repair yard in Key West—they brought with them the model of an ironclad warship designed by Nelson. The projected craft would have neither curves or rounded ends, so that, as Nelson said, even house carpenters could build it. Later the Tifts offered to arrange the construction of one or more "such vessels" without compensation except for travelling expense. The proposal accepted, the brothers proceeded to New Orleans and started construction of an ironclad based on Nelson's design. She was named the *Mississippi*.

By the end of August the Confederate naval secretary had authorized the construction of three powerful armored vessels in the West, and two weeks later he was negotiating for the building of a fourth. On September 18 E. C. Murray, a Kentuckian and an experienced boat-builder, contracted for an ironclad at New Orleans. The *Louisiana*, as Murray's vessel was named, was laid down the last week in September.

Mallory's policy of emphasizing the construction of ironclads was beginning to unfold. While not neglecting other types of vessels, the secretary declared throughout the war that he would "put his faith" in a few powerful ironclads. This policy was indicated in his report to the President:

> The judgment of naval men and of other experts in naval construction have, . . . been consulted [and] . . . it is believed, enable us with a small number of vessels comparatively to keep our waters free from the enemy and ultimately to contest with them the possession of his own. The two ironclad frigates at New Orleans, the two plated ships at Memphis . . . and the *Virginia* are vessels of this character.[13]

The five ironclads mentioned in this report were all unusually large in contrast to the later "home water" armored vessels and were designed to operate on the open sea as well as inland waters.

Not all Confederate naval officers shared Mallory's conviction that their best policy should be the construction of ironclads. On October 22, 1861, one of the most revered officers in Confederate naval service, Matthew Fontaine Maury, proposed the building of small wooden gunboats for river and harbor defense. Convinced that the South lacked facilities necessary to build large warships, including ironclads, he advocated the construction of small craft with "neither cabin, nor steerage, nor any accommodation on board." This Lilliputian fleet of steam gunboats, each 112 feet in length, 21 feet in beam, drawing 6 feet of water, and mounting two rifled pivot guns, was reminiscent of Thomas Jefferson's gunboats prior to the war of 1812. His proposal was sent to the Virginia Convention and forwarded to the Confederate Congress, where it was well received. Maury had a world-wide reputation and any proposal of his deserved consideration; moreover, his plan satisfied two requirements vital to the lawmakers—economy and time. The famed oceanographer estimated that one of his proposed wooden gunboats could be built in a few weeks for approximately $10,000. Shortly before Christmas of 1861 Congress passed a bill authorizing the construction of not more than one hundred of the small vessels recommended by Maury and appropriated two million dollars for the work.[14] Maury took charge of the project, and altogether fifteen of these vessels were laid down at yards on the Rappahannock, Pamunkey, and York Rivers, and in Norfolk. Only two of them, the *Hampton* and the *Nansemond*, reached completion; the others were burned on the stocks.

Curiously, Mallory developed a plan for a fleet of small gunboats at the same time that Maury was pushing his proposal. On November 26, 1861, William P. Williamson, Confederate chief engineer, wrote to a shipbuilder in North Carolina: "We are about to build a *large number* of gun boats to carry two guns each and shall probably get you to build several. Don't speak of this to anybody . . . as it is only known at this time to the Secretary and myself. They will be about 100 or 120 feet long, and 18 or 20 feet beam."[15] One week later he wrote to the same gentleman: "In regard to the 50 gun boats . . . Mr. Porter has made the drawings. They are 106 feet long, 21 feet beam and 8 feet deep. These designs have been accepted by the Secretary." More than likely these vessels had the same basic plan as Maury's 112 footers; Naval Constructor Porter, who probably drew up the plans, was notorious for lengthening or shortening the same design by adding or substracting at the midship section. The Navy Department contracted for at least five of these vessels, three to be built at Elizabeth City, North Carolina, and two in Early County, Georgia; but there is no evidence that any of them were completed.

The naval secretary also approved the construction of a number of larger wooden-hull gunboats in the fall of 1861: one 130-foot vessel in Saffold (early county), Georgia; nine 150-foot vessels (one each at Pensacola and Jacksonville, Florida, Elizabeth City, North Carolina, Mars Bluff, South Carolina; two at Savannah, Georgia; three in Washington, North Carolina); and two 196-foot vessels at Mobile, Alabama. Of these, the *Pee Dee*, built at Mars Bluff near Marion Courthouse, the *Macon* (ex-*Ogeechee*), built at Savannah, the *Chattahoochee*, built in Saffold County, Georgia, and the *Morgan* and *Gaines*, built in Mobile, were completed and commissioned. He sought builders in other localities such as St. Marks, Florida; Brunswick, Georgia; and Galveston, Texas, but without success.[16]

The *Pee Dee* and *Chattahoochee*, twin-screw steamers, contributed very little to the Southern war effort. The former was commissioned in April 1864 and was destroyed in the Pee Dee River near Georgetown, South Carolina, upon the evacuation of Charleston in February 1865, having never fired a shot in anger. The latter was completed early in 1863, but a boiler explosion a few months later so damaged her that she had to be laid up for extensive repairs. She became operational again just in time to be destroyed by her own crew in order to prevent capture by advancing Federal forces.

The other wooden gunboats were more successful. The *Macon*, completed in August 1864, participated in the defense of Savannah, and when that city fell she fled up the river to Augusta and remained there until the end of the war. The *Morgan* and *Gaines* were laid down in September 1861 and finished the following spring. One officer described the *Morgan* as "a perfect little beauty." The vessel's captain, however, was not so impressed: "Her engines, two in number, are high pressure and not sufficiently powerful to drive so large a hull with the requisite speed. Her steam pipes are entirely above the waterline, and her boilers and magazines partly above it. So we have the comfortable appearance of being blown up or scalded by any chance shot that may not take off our heads."[17] Nevertheless, the *Morgan* and her sister gunboat, the *Gaines*, performed well in the defense of Mobile Bay. The *Gaines* was run aground by her own officers during the engagement of August 5, 1864, to avoid capture by Admiral Farragut's fleet. The *Morgan* escaped that night and fought in the defense of the city until she was surrendered to Union forces in May 1865.

Little change occurred in the navy's shipbuilding program

during the early months of 1862; the conversion of riverboats, Maury's gunboat project, and construction of the wooden gunboats and ironclads proceeded apace. The *Merrimack's* transformation into an armorclad was rapidly approaching completion. Commissioned the *Virginia*, the ironclad elicited enthusiasm from Mallory. On February 27 he wrote in his report to the President that the five ironclads under construction and others of this type would be able "to keep our waters free from the enemy. . . ." Five days later he replied to an inquiry from the House of Representatives, "as to what additional means in money, men, arms, and the munitions of war are . . . necessary . . . for the public service" that fifty light-draft ironclads for local defense and four armored cruisers could be used immediately.[18]

No action had been taken on the recommendation when the *Virginia* fought her celebrated battle in Hampton Roads. It was this engagement that dramatically illustrated the justification of Mallory's faith in ironclad vessels-of-war. A few days after the conflict a Confederate naval officer wrote that "as to the wooden gunboats we are building, they are not worth a cent." Congress agreed completely with this sentiment. On March 17 the House of Representatives passed a resolution which declared it "of the utmost importance that this government should construct with the least possible delay as many small ironclad rams as practicable," authorizing the president to suspend the act approving the construction of Maury's wooden gunboats. From then on Mallory would make every effort to build up a powerful fleet of armored ships.

At first Mallory evidently favored converting Maury's wooden gunboats under construction into ironclads. However, after a series of conferences with various naval officers, on March 29 he recommended to the president that the wooden gunboats already on the stocks be completed as planned. At the same time he asked what remained of the two million dollars appropriated for Maury's vessels be transferred to the building of additional armored ships. On May 1 Congress gave Mallory the authorization he desired.

The secretary had not waited for congressional approval

to expand his ironclad program. In the latter part of February, Captain Duncan Ingraham, ranking Confederate naval officer in Charleston, was empowered to negotiate a contract for building a 150-foot harbor defense ironclad, which became the *Palmetto State*. On March 7 a shipbuilder in New Orleans received a contract to construct a large ironclad ram, and a few days later Commander John K. Mitchell (also in New Orleans) was ordered to engage builders for an unspecified number of the 150-foot class vessel. At the navy yard in Norfolk still another of this class was laid down. By May 1 Mallory sanctioned at least twelve new ironclads, either by contract or in navy yards.[19]

Although a few wooden vessels would be laid down from the spring of 1862 until the end of the war, naval building within the Confederacy would be concentrated on ironclads. Naval Constructor John Porter on March 3, 1863, testified before a congressional committee that of twenty-three gunboats at that time under construction in the Confederacy, twenty were ironclad and three wooden. Altogether, between August 1861 and January 1863, the Navy Department closed thirty-one contracts with firms or individuals at various points within the Confederacy for the construction of some forty wooden gunboats and ironclads. The department laid down in navy yards an undetermined number of vessels.[20] In addition to naval building under the direction of the Navy Department, the War Department, several state governments, and private citizens also engaged in ship construction.

The Confederate government entered the war with no policy defining the relationship between the army and navy in the overall strategy of defense. This vagueness in the command system which continued throughout the conflict was to result in many instances of misunderstanding and friction between the two service branches. Early in the war when there were more naval officers than ships for them to man, many officers were assigned to army commanders to take charge of batteries and small craft when they were available. In several instances military commanders attempted to use these naval subordinates to create naval forces or to take charge of gunboats under their control. This was particularly true in the West where the command structure was even more confused because of the peculiar nature of river warfare.

In the fall of 1861, General Leonidas Polk, in command of Confederate forces in western Tennessee, decided to form a river defense flotilla. On October 15 he wrote to Mallory: "I am very much in need of . . . boats to operate upon the Mississippi, Tennessee, and Cumberland rivers. I can purchase one on the Mississippi River . . . for $20,000; one on the Tennessee for $12,000; and another on the Cumberland River for about the same amount. These can speedily be converted into armed gunboats. . . ."[21] A naval lieutenant attached to his command had already converted the steamer *Edward Howard* into a gunboat named the *General Polk*. On October 31 the steamer *Eastport* was purchased, towed to Cerro Gordo on the Tennessee River, and razed to her main deck for conversion into an ironclad gunboat. The work was never completed—at least not by the Confederates—for in February 1862 she was captured by Union forces, completed as an ironclad, and attached to the Mississippi Squadron until her destruction during the 1864 Red River expedition. Polk's request in October to purchase four steamers was approved, and they were laid up in Nashville for conversion. However, before completion the advance of Federal troops necessitated their destruction.

The War Department attempted also to form a naval force in Texas. Commander William W. Hunter, CSN, was sent to Texas for this purpose, and helped to create the "Texas Marine Department, Confederate States Army." From September 1861 until the end of the war more than twenty-five ships were commissioned by the Marine Department. Few of them, however, were converted into gunboats and none were built from the keel up.[22]

In terms of numbers the most successful effort by the War Department to develop a naval force occurred on the lower Mississippi where early in 1862 General Mansfield Lovell seized fourteen steamers by order of Secretary of War

Judah P. Benjamin. The seized vessels, Benjamin wrote, will "not be part of the Navy . . . [but] will be subject to the general command of the military chief of the department. . . ."[23] Thirteen of them were converted into gunboats and became known as the "River Defense Fleet." Vessels from this fleet participated in three river engagements. They won the Battle of Plum Point Bend, failed the Confederacy at New Orleans, and met with defeat off Memphis.

Army involvement in naval construction was not limited to the West. General P. G. T. Beauregard, while in command of the Department of South Carolina and Georgia from September 1862 to April 1864, approved and strongly encouraged the building of a war vessel by one of his officers. Beauregard, who believed in a unified command with naval forces operating under his control, was extremely critical of the warships, particularly ironclad, that comprised the naval squadron at Charleston.

Captain Francis D. Lee, an ingenious young engineer in Beauregard's command, developed a torpedo which attached to a long pole or spar would explode upon contact with the hull of a ship. In order to carry this weapon to the enemy, he designed also a semi-submergible vessel with only the smokestack, pilot's cockpit, and top of the armored hull breaking above the water. Beauregard was enthusiastic about the project. Although he received little support from the navy (except an unfinished gunboat hull), he did get approval from the War Department and funds from the state of South Carolina. The "torpedo ram," as it was called, was completed except for its armor, but failed in its two attacks on Union vessels.[24]

Lee claimed also to have designed the original *David*—similar in appearance to his "torpedo ram," but much smaller. However, the *David* may have been a private venture which was turned over to the navy upon completion. When she torpedoed the *New Ironsides* off Charleston Harbor, the Navy Department recommended the construction of similar cigar-shaped vessels in various ports throughout the Confederacy. Beauregard ordered additional ones built at Charleston and Wilmington and placed Lee in charge of the project. Although a large number of these small vessels were laid down, very few were completed. Certainly none equalled the success of the original *David*.[25]

State governments, conscious of their vulnerable coastlines, made efforts to provide vessels for defense. As mentioned earlier, they commissioned several small steamers and turned them over to the Confederate government. In addition, several states attempted to build warships. The Mississippi legislature appropriated $50,000 for the building of light-draft gunboats; the Tennessee legislature petitioned Congress to authorize the construction of river gunboats for defense of the Cumberland and Tennessee Rivers; the Louisiana legislature debated a resolution to allocate funds for gunboat construction; the Alabama General Assembly on November 8, 1861, passed an act appropriating $150,000 for the "construction of an iron clad gunboat and ram for the defense of the bay and harbor of Mobile," and in December the South Carolina General Assembly set up a special committee to investigate the possibility of building war vessels.

Five gunboats were eventually completed: two (the *Governor Moore* and *General Quitman*) by Louisiana, two by South Carolina (ironclads *Chicora* and *Charleston*), and the ironclad *Baltic* by the state of Alabama. The *Governor Moore* (the coastwise steamer *Charles Morgan* before conversion) was a cottonclad: only her bow was reinforced by iron straps for ramming. The *General Quitman*, formerly the *Galveston*, was the same type but smaller than the *Morgan*. Both vessels were destroyed when New Orleans fell in April 1862.

The three ironclads built by Alabama and South Carolina were turned over to the Confederate government. The *Baltic* was converted from a lighter used to transport cotton from Mobile to ships in the lower bay. She was completed in May 1862, and for the next two years was the only armored vessel to defend the bay. Her bottom had not been protected with copper sheeting and was so worm-eaten by 1864 that she was no longer seaworthy; "rotten as punk, and . . . about as fit to go into action as a mud scow," wrote her commanding officer.

Most of her armor was then stripped off to be used on another ironclad under construction.[26]

Early in 1862 South Carolina appropriated $300,000 for the construction of an ironclad. The ironclad *Chicora* was completed in the fall of 1862 and joined the Confederate squadron defending Charleston. Later a more powerful armored vessel, the *Charleston*, was built under the authority of the state. They were blown up when the city was evacuated by Confederate forces in February 1865.

Very little shipbuilding was carried out in the South during the Civil War other than for naval purposes. The few private yards and experienced builders were under contract with the navy throughout the conflict. There is little evidence that vessels for private use, including blockade runners, were built.[27]

The Confederate government issued letters of marque and reprisal in 1861, and a number of privateers were fitted out. Two of these ships, both built in New Orleans, were unusual. A group of the city's residents attempted to build submarines for privateering. The *Pioneer*, completed in the spring of 1862, had a test run on Lake Pontchartrain. The Confederate government awarded a letter of marque to the *Pioneer* in March 1862, but the vessel was lost before she could begin operations. The builders moved on to Mobile where they built a second one which sank while attempting to attack the blockading squadron off Mobile Bay. They then constructed a third submergible, later named the CSS *H. L. Hunley* after one of the builders. Carried to Charleston on a flatcar, the *Hunley*, after several tragic failures, succeeded in sinking the Union warship *Housatonic*.[28]

The armored vessel *Manassas* was also a privateering project of a number of New Orleans citizens. With the encouragement of the Confederate government they purchased the river towboat *Enoch Train* (selected because of her heavily-constructed bow) for conversion into an ironclad. In the shipyard her masts and superstructure were removed, and a convex iron shield was built over the main deck. The bow was lengthened, and a heavy cast iron ram attached below the water line. Shortly after these modifications were finished in the fall of 1861, Confederate naval officials in New Orleans commandeered her for a contemplated attack against the Union blockaders at the mouth of the Mississippi River. She remained a commissioned naval vessel until she was destroyed on April 24 while defending New Orleans against Farragut.

From 1861 to 1865 the Confederate government, state governments, and private concerns converted, contracted for, or laid down in the Southern states at least 150 warships. Less than a third of them reached operational status. The remainder were not completed, primarily because of the magnitude and complexity of the problems faced by a predominantly agricultural section.

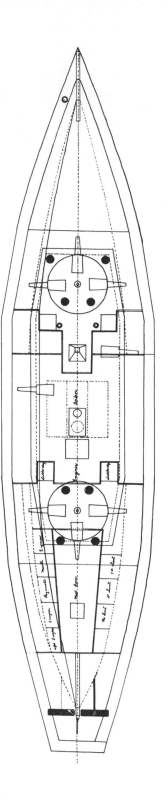

Facilities

WHEN WAR broke out in 1861, the Confederate states did not then have the facilities necessary to construct or equip vessels-of-war.[1] Shipyards of adequate size were scarce, as were plants for the manufacture of iron plate, marine machinery, and ordnance. Secretary Mallory and his colleagues were well aware of the deficiencies, but clung to the optimistic belief that adequate facilities could be established.

Of the ten navy yards operated by the United States government in 1860, two were in the South: one at Norfolk, the other at Pensacola. The smaller was the Pensacola yard, which was primarily a coaling and refitting station. Nevertheless, two large sloops (the *Pensacola* of over 2,000 tons and the *Seminole* of 800 tons) were built there during the 1850s. At the Gosport Navy Yard in Norfolk, thirteen warships, including four screw steamers, had come off the ways before 1861. Both yards were obviously important in Confederate plans for the construction of war vessels.

There were also a few large, privately-owned shipyards and many small yards in operation. The exact number is difficult to determine because of frequent abandonment and new construction. Most of them were rather simple affairs—a small clear area on a beach, the bank of a river, a creek, or an inlet. They required only water deep enough for launching and readily-available timber and other materials. According to the 1860 census on manufacturing, there were thirty-six yards in the states that were to form the Confederacy. This census figure, however, is questionable. There were no yards listed in Mississippi, for example, yet there were small establishments at Pearlington and Gainesville on the Mississippi River. There were none listed for either Tennessee or Texas, although in the 1850s there were at least eight steam merchant vessels built in Tennessee and ten in Texas. One writer in 1850 estimated that the South, including Maryland, Kentucky, and the area that became West Virginia, had 145 shipyards. Although there was a decline in Southern shipbuilding in the decade of the 1850s, the total number of Southern yards lay somewhere between the estimated 1850 figure of 145 and the 1860 figure of 36.

In the United States as a whole slightly over 8,000 vessels of wood or iron were constructed between 1849 and 1858. Of this number Southern shipyards built approximately 1,600. Steam vessels were constructed in all the Southern states, and the places which were construction centers before the war became the first centers of shipbuilding in the Confederacy. The most important centers were Norfolk, Charleston, Savannah, Mobile, and New Orleans—coastal towns which were also the most important shipping ports. Nevertheless, other smaller towns—not only seaports but river towns—became important construction centers, particularly after the capture of Norfolk and New Orleans in the spring and summer of 1862. Mallory realized the unsuitability of some of the new locations for building large sea-going steamers, but by that time the strategy of defense was dominant. What he wanted and needed were shallow-draft vessels capable of navigating in the shoal waters of the South. These vessels, including ironclads, should be flat-bottomed, of slight draft, and simple to construct—the type of vessel which small shipyards of limited means could turn out.

Related industries, such as those for the manufacture of iron, marine machinery, and ordnance, were in short supply in the South when war began. There was little problem if ships were to be made of wood, since the South had an adequate supply of sawmills, and nearly every community or large plantation possessed a mill for cutting timber, but mills for the manufacture of iron were limited. In 1860 the South had ninety-six foundries and eighty-two rolling mills or other establishments that produced bar, sheet, and railroad iron. Most of these establishments were small-scale. There were only eleven rolling mills of any size: five in Virginia, three in South Carolina, one in Georgia, and two in Tennessee. Furthermore, at the outbreak of war, none of these was able to roll two-inch plate. Virginia was by far the most important Southern state in the manufacture of iron products, but in contrast with Pennsylvania, the leading state in the United States, its production was quite small.

The availability of adequate facilities for manufacturing ship machinery is difficult to determine. Shortly after the outbreak of hostilities, Mallory wrote that Tennessee was the only state which had factories capable of producing complete engines. But he was mistaken. Of the steamships built in Norfolk before the war, two of them had engines (complete except for their shafts) made in the Tredegar Iron Works in Richmond. In addition, by 1860 there were nearly a hundred shops, large and small, which had built and repaired steam engines. The census figures, unfortunately, do not indicate the type of machinery. Other sources make clear, however, that there were a number of large foundries in the South making marine engines, such as the Nobles Foundry of Rome, Georgia; the Leeds Company and the Clarke Foundry of New Orleans; Skates and Company of Mobile; and the Shockoe Foundry of Richmond. There were also machine shops and foundries in the river towns and seaports where shipping was a major industry. Nevertheless, the lack of suitable facilities for producing marine machinery proved to be a serious weakness in the Confederate shipbuilding program.

Tredegar was the only establishment in the South that cast naval ordnance before the war. Between 1844 and 1860 the company cast and delivered a total of 881 pieces of ordnance to the Federal government.[2] Although Tredegar manufactured some shot and shell, facilities for ordnance stores were almost nonexistent in Southern states, with the exception of two small powder mills.

Thus at the outbreak of the Civil War there were a number of facilities in the Confederate states available to support a navy, but the value or importance of the facilities was not uniform. The obvious interdependence of the naval industries increased the magnitude of the South's problem. The Confederacy might develop adequate plants for casting guns, rolling plate, and manufacturing machinery, but they were useless unless sufficient iron was available. In addition, the various naval establishments were to compete with each other, as well as with other industries, throughout the war for raw materials, transportation, and labor. Given more time, this competition might not have proven so disastrous, but the Confederacy was born in war with an urgent need to create its own navy.

In the old United States navy all yards came under the Bureau of Yards and Docks, and ship construction was the responsibility of the Bureau of Construction, Equipment, and Repair. The senior naval officer in charge of the latter bureau was responsible for initiating the navy's shipbuilding program as laid out by the secretary of the navy and approved by Congress. When the Confederate Navy Department was organized, four bureaus were set up,[3] but there was no bureau of construction, equipment, and repair or its equivalent. In fact, the Confederate naval secretary retained direct control of the navy's shipbuilding program throughout the war. In 1862 semi-autonomous positions were created to handle specific aspects of the program: William P. Williamson was appointed engineer-in-chief and John L. Porter was appointed chief naval constructor. Although these positions were basically administrative, Mallory himself continued to initiate ship construction. Plans, proposals, and ideas came to him for consideration, and he made the decision on their adoption. He frequently consulted various naval officers, particularly Porter,

Williamson, and Lieutenant John M. Brooke, before making a final decision.

The details of construction and the supervision of the program in the various yards, both private and public, were within the province of Porter and the "acting constructors" under him. Porter was not only responsible for the designs of a majority of the warships laid down by the Confederate government, but also the steering apparatus, decks, interior furnishings, small boats, etc. In the fall of 1861 Porter confided to a friend: "I never was so busy in all my life. I have all the work in the [Gosport] navy yard to direct, and all the duties of the Bureau of Construction. I have all the planning of the various gun boats to do which are being built all over the South. . . . The Secretary refers most of the matter concerning the building of vessels, buying materials, etc., to me." Porter and his assistants, William A. Graves and Joseph Pierce, made frequent trips to inspect construction in progress and to make recommendations.

Chief Engineer Williamson, a Virginian and veteran of the United States navy—one of the first to be appointed when the engineering branch was established in 1842—was responsible for furnishing engineering designs (engines, boilers, etc.) for ships under construction, as well as supervising their trial and inspection runs.

Ordnance, ordnance stores, storage, and navigation instruments fell to the authority of the Office of Ordnance and Hydrography, while the office of Orders and Detail saw to anchor gear, coal and water storage, sails, and masts.[4]

Mallory followed three plans in his shipbuilding program: (1) construction of ships in navy yards under direct supervision of the department; (2) authorization of departmental agents to supervise the building of vessels; (3) contract with private yards for Confederate vessels. A large majority of the vessels constructed, or at least laid down, in the Confederacy were built by contract. This does not reflect necessity, as some writers have emphasized, but was the prevailing economic philosophy of the Confederacy. The Confederate

government was not generally interested in developing shipbuilding or other industries of its own, and tried many
ways—including bonuses, government subsidization of new industries, and advancing money to encourage private industry.
The government did attempt to regulate profits, labor, and
transportation in private industry. Shipbuilding under contract was, generally speaking, controlled throughout the war.
In a few instances ships under construction were taken
over completely by the department, but in most cases naval
officers were ordered to assist the contractors in fulfilling
their obligations.

The shipbuilding program got underway early, with
wooden vessels and ironclads under construction in both
government and private shipyards. Most of the early contracts
were with experienced builders who already had the necessary
facilities and equipment. Arrangements were made to construct or convert vessels at New Orleans, Memphis, Nashville,
Mobile, Jacksonville, Savannah, Charleston, Wilmington,
Washington (North Carolina), and Norfolk. Ships were also
laid down directly under the supervision of the Navy Department at yards in Norfolk, Pensacola, New Orleans, and along
the Pamunkey, Rappahannock, and York Rivers in Virginia.
By the end of the first year of the war there were at least
eighteen yards building vessels for the navy.

Norfolk was the most important shipbuilding center in
the Confederacy. In addition to the Gosport Navy Yard,
which prior to the war had been one of the best equipped in
the United States, there were a number of private yards. The
navy yard lay above the cities of Norfolk and Portsmouth on
the Portsmouth side of Elizabeth River. For building or re-
pairing ships the yard contained a dry dock, two large ship
houses and a third under construction, sail lofts, rigger's
lofts, gunner's lofts, sawmills, timber sheds, spar houses, car-
penter shops, foundries, machine shops, boiler shops, and an
ordnance store and laboratory. In April 1861 Union forces
withdrew from the city and partially destroyed the yard. The
Confederate Navy Department quickly rebuilt the facility,

however, and started repairs on the miscellaneous captured naval craft, including the sloop *Merrimack*.[5]

New Orleans and Memphis were the logical sites at which to establish naval shipyards in the West. In 1819 the first shipyard with marine ways was established in New Orleans. From that time until the outbreak of the war the city was a center of steamboat construction. The census of 1860 shows Louisiana with ten shipyards and two additional establishments for "ship carpentering," at least five of which were in New Orleans. By April 1862 they had constructed, converted, or had begun work on more than thirty vessels-of-war.[6]

Memphis had been the site of a navy yard. In 1842 Matthew F. Maury wrote an article in the *National Intelligencer* suggesting the city for a naval establishment. Although Congress approved and the yard was established in 1844, only one warship was constructed before it was deactivated and the buildings sold in the 1850s.[7] Nevertheless, because of the city's industrial facilities as well as strategic importance, two ironclads were laid down in the fall of 1861 at Fort Pickering, a landing below the city.

These vessels were still on the ways when the first great military disaster to the Southern cause occurred. On February 16, 1862, Fort Donelson in northwestern Tennessee surrendered to a small Union army under General Ulysses S. Grant. This victory cleared the way for an invasion of central Tennessee and forced Confederate General Albert Sidney Johnston to give up his defensive line along the Tennessee-Kentucky border and fall back into northern Mississippi. A new defensive line was established from Corinth in northeast Mississippi to Island Number Ten in the Mississippi River and New Madrid on the Missouri side. This line collapsed in April with the Confederate defeat at Shiloh on the sixth and the capitulation of Island Number Ten two days later. With a Federal army in Corinth, Memphis was doomed. On June 6 a naval force of rams and gunboats under Flag Officer Charles Davis destroyed a Confederate fleet within sight of hundreds of Memphis citizens, who lined the bluffs to see the spectacle, and forced the defenseless city to surrender. Federal forces found the burned remains of one ironclad still on the stocks. Confederate officials had ordered the destruction of the vessel on the stocks and the removal of a second one, the *Arkansas*, to a safer place six weeks before when news of the fall of New Orleans reached Memphis. The *Arkansas* was towed to Yazoo City, Mississippi, and completed.

While Union forces were coming down the upper Mississippi, a naval squadron under Flag Officer David G. Farragut had concentrated off the delta passes to the Mississippi River. On the night of April 24 Farragut's vessels passed the forts guarding the river approach to New Orleans and captured the city. Confederate naval forces on the lower Mississippi, including the ironclads *Louisiana*, *Manassas*, and *Mississippi* were destroyed.

The surrender of New Orleans not only resulted in the destruction of the Confederate ironclad at Mississippi but also the loss of the navy yard at Pensacola. Colonel Thomas M. Jones, CSA, commanding at Pensacola, reported: "On receiving information that the enemy's gunboats had succeeded in passing the forts below New Orleans with their powerful batteries and splendid equipment, I came to the conclusion that, with my limited means of defense, reduced, as I have been by the withdrawal of nearly all my heavy guns and ammunition, I could not hold them in check or make even a respectable show of resistance."[8] On May 10 the city was evacuated after military installations, including the navy yard and the nearly-repaired gunboat *Fulton*, were destroyed.

Union combined operations were equally successful on the east coast. On March 14, New Bern, North Carolina, was captured by a force under General Ambrose Burnside as a base from which to threaten Richmond. Early in May Norfolk was evacuated by Confederate forces, losing to the navy not only its most important shipbuilding facility, but also the *Virginia*. The ironclad was blown up when it was discovered that she drew too much water to be brought up the James River. The loss of the *Virginia* opened the way for Union

General George McClellan to begin his Peninsula campaign with Richmond as its ultimate objective.

The loss of New Orleans, Memphis, and Norfolk, along with Nashville in February, Jacksonville (Florida) and New Bern in March, and Pensacola in May, were disasters for Mallory's shipbuilding program. Not only were a large number of vessels under construction destroyed, but irreplaceable stores and equipment were lost. As a result of these setbacks a significant change occurred in the location of Confederate naval establishments. Up to that time most naval industries were concentrated in the large coastal and river ports, but from the summer of 1862 they were located in the interior whenever possible. To do so provided more security from attack, but it had the serious disadvantage of deconcentration. No single facility possessed everything needed to construct and outfit a vessel. Shipyards were in various localities; ordnance stores and laboratories in others; and foundries, machine shops, iron works, and ropewalks were in still other locations. Transportation was obviously essential, but transportation within the Confederacy, particularly railroads, was never adequate; and as the war progressed the railroads became increasingly inefficient, seriously affecting the naval building program. A majority of the railroads were small separate lines with different gauges. There was a serious shortage of operating equipment and rails which continued to deteriorate because of lack of replacements. Skilled labor was scarce and the competition between the Confederate government and the various state governments for use of the rails all contributed to the mounting chaos.

Even during the first year of the war the completion of warships was delayed because of transportation difficulties. The armor plate for the ironclad *Virginia*, under conversion at Norfolk, was rolled in the last three months of 1861 and the first month of 1862 by the Tredegar works in Richmond. As the plates came off the lines ready for shipment the Navy Department requested rail transportation to Norfolk. Early in October the Richmond and Petersburg Railroad Company was asked to ship "some 70 to 100 tons of the [*Virginia's*] iron now ready. . . ." The railroad could not comply immediately, for flatcars were not available.[9] Approximately one-thousand tons of armor plate were needed for the ironclad, but only two-hundred tons reached the yard in October. Under urgent appeals from the naval constructor in charge as well as from Mallory, who made several trips to the rolling mill to "encourage work," Tredegar's president wrote that he was forwarding the bow and stern iron as "rapidly as we can get it transported."[10] In order to expedite the shipments, the company began routing some of the plates over the Richmond and Danville Railroad to Burkeville, and from there via the Southside Railroad to Petersburg. This eased but did not solve the problem. "We have iron for the Navy Yard that has been lying on the bank for 4 weeks," a member of the company wrote in mid-November. Two weeks later the worried Navy Department arranged for the Petersburg Railroad to carry it to Weldon, North Carolina, where it was transferred to the Seaboard and Roanoke Railroad and taken to Norfolk.

Tredegar was the only foundry in the Confederacy with the facilities to re-work the main shaft for the ironclad *Mississippi* then under construction in New Orleans. When completed, a special railroad car was built to carry it to New Orleans. Although the loaded car began its long journey in March 1862, it arrived in New Orleans in mid-April, nearly a month later and only a few days before the city fell.[11]

Despite the Confederate government's increasing control over the railroads, the navy found its use curtailed because of army control. Mallory, naval officers, builders, and contractors constantly complained, with some justification, that the army ignored their requirements. For example, Captain William F. Lynch, CSN, reported to the secretary of the navy that "Fourteen car loads of plate iron arrived last evening, and for a week past we have had two car loads waiting transportation to Kinston and Halifax [North Carolina]. The whole rolling capacity of the road, except passenger trains, has been monopolized by the army, and I fear the completion of the gun boats at those places will be delayed."[12]

The destruction of a great many ironclads and other vessels while they were still under construction was at least partially a result of the serious transportation problems.

The new interior sites (some of which were not connected by railroad lines) included Richmond, Virginia; Edward's Ferry and Whitehall, North Carolina; Mars Bluff, South Carolina; Saffold and Columbus, Georgia; Yazoo City, Mississippi; Selma, Montgomery, and Oven Bluff, Alabama; and Shreveport, Louisiana. At Richmond the yard known as Rocketts was chosen as a navy yard. Although described by one naval officer as nothing more than a "shed with 200 or 300 carpenters," three ironclads were completed and others were laid down at this facility. In North Carolina Gilbert Elliott and William P. Martin received contracts to build both ironclads and wooden gunboats; only one of these, the *Albemarle*, constructed at Edward's Ferry, reached operational status. A sister ship, the *Neuse*, was completed at Whitehall. Wooden gunboats were laid down at Mars Bluff, South Carolina, and Saffold, Georgia, while the ironclad *Jackson* [*Muscogee*] was finished at Columbus, Georgia. Yazoo City became the site of a yard, not by design but because the unfinished *Arkansas* was towed there from a shipyard near Memphis. Here the Navy Department took over and finished her under a naval officer's supervision. Later a large ironclad ram was laid down, and a small wooden steamer was stripped for conversion into an armored vessel, but they were never completed.[13] At Oven Bluff, Alabama, some sixty miles up the Tombigbee River from Mobile, the wooden hulls of three ironclads were built, but the incompetence of the contractors and the deleterious effect of the malaria-ridden swamp on workers prevented the completion of the vessels. Towed later to Mobile, they were still without armor and machinery when the city surrendered in the spring of 1865. The keels of four ironclads were laid down at Selma, but only three (*Tuscaloosa*, *Huntsville*, and *Tennessee*) were completed. The Confederate government purchased four river steamers and placed them in yards in Nashville, Tennessee, for conversion into gunboats, they were destroyed when that city was evacuated in

February 1862. Nine ironclads and one wooden gunboat were commissioned at these inland yards; at least fourteen others, including eight ironclads, were destroyed before becoming operational.[14]

The trans-Mississippi West presented more numerous problems in establishing naval facilities. With the exception of a yard at Shreveport, where the ironclad *Missouri* was built, and several small yards in Texas, where wooden gunboats were converted from merchant steamers, little was accomplished. President Davis, who usually showed little interest in naval matters, became concerned about the lack of naval vessels in the West. General Edmund Kirby Smith was ordered to investigate the possibility of constructing gunboats and marine machinery at Little Rock, Arkansas. In 1863 a naval constructor sent to Texas to ascertain whether ironclads could be built there reported that materials were not available.

The availability of materials anywhere in the Confederacy, and particularly the availability of iron for armor plate, continuously hindered the shipbuilding program. Four out of every five ships built in the Confederacy after the spring of 1862 were ironclads, and the acquisition of armor plate for these vessels was a continuing difficulty. At the outset of the war there were no rolling mills within the South capable of producing two-inch plate, and during the course of the war only three appeared: Tredegar Iron Works and the Scofield & Markham Iron Works converted their machinery in 1861, and the Shelby Iron Company of Columbiana, Alabama, followed in 1863. The department attempted to increase the number of rolling mills capable of producing two-inch plate, but without success.[15]

Tredegar Iron Works was the most important industrial establishment in the Confederacy.[16] The company manufactured ordnance, ordnance stores, railroad equipment and rails, and various iron parts for warships, including machinery and armor plate. In July 1861 the president of Tredegar agreed to roll the armor plate for the *Virginia*. The first contract called for one-inch plate, but a series of experiments conducted by the navy on Jamestown Island resulted in the decision to use two-inch plate instead of one-inch. Tredegar agreed to modify their rollers and in early September manufactured the first two-inch plates. From then until hostilities ended, the Richmond works rolled plate for the navy. Immediately after the completion of the *Virginia* in early 1862, the Tredegar rolling mills started producing the iron plates for the *Richmond*, also on the way at the navy yard in Norfolk. When Confederate forces evacuated the port in May, the *Richmond* was towed up the James River and completed at Rocketts. Later the *Virginia II*, *Fredericksburg*, and several of the North Carolina ironclads received their armor from the Richmond plant, but the lack of iron for armor delayed completion of the latter vessel until late 1863, and the others until 1864.

In November the president of Tredegar wrote to one of his customers: "We are now pressed almost beyond endurance for the heavy iron work to complete one of the war vessels *now ready for operations.* . . . It is a most fortunate thing that we could render this assistance to our little Navy—It could not have been done elsewhere in the Confederacy."[17] This assertion was not completely true for at that time the builders of the *Mississippi* in New Orleans were negotiating with Scofield and Markham of Atlanta to convert their machinery in order to roll two-inch plate. By December the Atlanta firm was rolling plates at the rate of 150 per day. Until Atlanta was burned in 1864, the works continued to operate and provided the armor for at least ten ironclads.

The Shelby Iron Company was the only other establishment to roll armor plate for the navy. On September 1, 1862, Flag Officer William F. Lynch wrote the president of Shelby, Albert T. Jones, about producing plate for the navy. Jones agreed to do so, although he was under contract with the War Department at that time "to deliver the entire proceeds of the work [sic] up to 12,000 tons per year." Rolled plate, however, was more profitable than pig iron or bar iron, and Jones apparently believed that he could fulfill a naval order without breaking his contract with the ordnance bureau of the War Department. After discussions held in Richmond, Jones received a contract on September 27 for four hundred tons of two-inch plate. The agreement stipulated that delivery was to be on or before December 1, 1862.

The company then found itself in difficulty. In the first place, Shelby required additional machinery in order to roll two-inch plate. Jones promised to obtain the necessary equipment and to begin operations by the middle of December—a two-week delay. He also became involved in a dispute with the Confederate iron agent for Alabama, Colin J. McRae. McRae was not informed of the order he had negotiated, and found out about it only when his requisitions for iron were not filled. On November 5 he wrote to Jones angrily protesting the Lynch contract: "You are not the proper party to decide the necessity of the government. If such authority rests anywhere outside of the Department charged with making contracts, it would in this instance be with me as I have been appointed by the proper authority."[18] Two days later he wrote to Colonel Josiah Gorgas, commander of the army's ordnance bureau: "I have been made to play a most ridiculous part in the business and I again ask to be relieved from acting as the agent of the Department."[19] Evidently the trouble was resolved, for the Lynch order retained its priority, and McRae continued as iron agent until early in 1863 when he left on a mission to Europe.

The sixteen-hundred tons of plate ordered from Shelby for ironclads under construction at Yazoo City were never delivered. Shelby was still unable to roll the iron when the contract date (December 14) passed. Two days after Christmas, Commander Ebenezer Farrand, directing the building of two ironclads at Selma, informed an agent of the company that the Selma vessels were nearly ready for armor and that they would have priority over the Yazoo ships. The first plates were rolled early in March, and on the thirteenth Major William R. Hunt of the Niter and Mining Bureau ordered all orders suspended until the plate for the Selma boats was completed. The suspension order included the Lynch contract. Shelby continued to supply the navy with iron, although little armor plate was rolled because most of the iron was used for casting guns.

The first iron contracts made by the Confederate government called for delivery to be at a given date, but the agreements were rarely kept. Scarcity of iron made them impossible to carry out. By 1863 a new iron policy was adopted in the Confederacy whereby contractors and shipbuilders were to provide their own iron ore, scrap iron, or railroad iron to be manufactured into plate. When this also proved unworkable, the department began sending agents throughout the Confederacy searching for iron, and adopted a policy requiring the mills to roll into plate all of the iron the navy was able to obtain. Nevertheless, the production of plate iron was never adequate. On March 31, 1863, Tredegar temporarily closed down its mills because of an iron shortage. In November 1864 Mallory reported to the President that five ironclads were still unfinished because of insufficient iron for armor. The chief naval constructor, in his report of that month, stated that there were twelve ironclads awaiting plating. He also made it clear that the rolling mills were available, "but the material is not on hand."

A related "iron industry" vital to the naval shipbuilding program was marine machinery. In August 1862 Mallory asked Chief Engineer Williamson why there had been no progress in developing facilities for manufacturing marine machinery. Williamson's reply listed everything from insufficient labor to the scarcity of tools, but ended on the encouraging note that the situation would improve in the near future. His report reflected the unsatisfactory condition of the industry at that time. Some effort was made to stimulate the manufacture of ship machinery, but little was accomplished. The building of steam engines and other machinery required experienced and skilled mechanics, and very few of them were available; in addition, the tools and equipment needed to produce the engine parts had to be made or brought in through the blockade. Preparations were made to build marine machinery at the Norfolk yard, but the preparations were still incomplete when the evacuation took place. Mallory contracted also with various firms in New Orleans, Charleston, and other places, but the results were unsatisfactory.

Some progress was made in 1862. In February the navy leased the Shockoe Foundry at Richmond. This firm, which had equipment including a fitting shop, turning shop, foundry, and boiler shop, had made steam machinery before the war. It was secured to build machinery for small wooden gunboats. Later, after the construction of these vessels was dropped, the foundry produced power plants for ironclads. Tredegar also built machinery for ironclads: the *Richmond, Fredericksburg,* and *Virginia II* received all of their iron work, including power and propulsion plants, from these works.

In spite of these measures, however, a large percentage of the warships built or converted in the Confederate states received their machinery from river boats and other vessels. This was considered a temporary measure; the plan was to replace the old power plants with new ones when they became available. Unfortunately, the inland movement of machine shops along with shipbuilding facilities delayed the industry even further.

Charlotte, North Carolina, became the location of an important marine engineering works. In fact it was the only navy yard (after the fall of Norfolk) with the equipment for heavy forging. The Charlotte works did not manufacture complete engines, but many of the parts and nearly all of the shafts, propellers, and anchors were made there. The navy obtained a Nasmyth steam hammer from Tredegar at the beginning of the war and installed it at Charlotte.

Late in March 1862 the Office of Ordnance and Hydrography ordered an officer to Columbus, Georgia, to investigate the city's "general fitness for the location of extensive government works." Columbus had been an important industrial center before the war. One of its largest activities was the Columbus Iron Works, a firm engaged in the manufacture of steam machinery. On the opening of hostilities this company contracted with the War Department to cast small cannon, but in 1862 the Navy Department acquired control of the works. At first the navy planned to continue ordnance work, but in the summer of 1862 it was decided to use the facility to manufacture marine machinery. The establishment was then transferred to the Engineering Bureau and placed under the control of Chief Engineer James H. Warner, an experienced and capable officer. Extensive work was then done in expanding the plant; additional land was leased from the city, a small rolling mill and boiler plant were erected, tools and machinery designed by Warner were made at the works; and additional skilled labor, including a large number of Negroes, was hired. By October the engines for several vessels were in various stages of completion, in spite of the fact that the facility was still not operating on a full-scale basis. The works continued to expand until they became the most important plant in the Confederacy for the manufacture of marine machinery.

The navy's only ropewalk was located at Petersburg, Virginia. It began production in January 1863 and produced enough cotton rope, tarred cotton (a substitue for marlin or tarred hemp needed for standing rigging on sailing vessels), and other cordage to supply the needs of the army and navy and still have some available to sell to civilians for use in coal mines, railroads, and canal companies.[20] In the spring of 1864 Grant, who had been appointed supreme commander of the Federal armies, began his campaign in Virginia to destroy Lee's army. After a series of vicious battles the two armies faced each other at Petersburg. Late in June Grant started siege operations after his attempts to take the city by assault had failed. The siege would continue for nine months and would only end when the ragged survivors of Lee's army began their last march, which would halt at Appomattox Court House. The ropewalk operated until it became apparent that the Confederates would have to give up the city. In February 1865 Congress passed a bill appropriating $75,000 to remove it to another locality, but the move was not completed before the city was evacuated.

The last major part of the shipbuilding program was the manufacture and procurement of naval ordnance. Of all the bureaus under the direction of the naval secretary, that of Ordnance and Hydrography probably had the widest range of responsibilities. In addition to the procurement of ordnance and ordnance stores, this office was the one responsible for obtaining iron and other metals needed by the navy. Three officers were successively in charge of the bureau. The first, Duncan M. Ingraham, had been chief of the Bureau of Ordnance and Hydrography in the United States navy from 1856 until 1860, but had held the position in the Confederate navy only a short period, before assuming command of the squadron at Charleston. He relinquished the office to George Minor who had served as his assistant. Commander Minor was a capable, efficient officer who deserves much of the credit for organizing the bureau and creating the various naval ordnance establishments throughout the Confederacy. Little or nothing had been done by his predecessor toward organizing the office or establishing ordnance facilities, partly because the navy at that time had more than enough ordnance for its few ships. The evacuation of Norfolk by the Federals on April 20, 1861, resulted in the Confederate navy's obtaining over a thousand pieces of heavy ordnance, including some three-hundred Dahlgrens of the latest type. By the middle of July over 500 of these guns had been shipped to all parts of the Confederacy and, until the Brooke guns began to appear, this ordnance was the principal source for arming Confederate warships. In March 1863 John Mercer Brooke replaced Minor.

Brooke was undoubtedly one of the most capable of the old navy officers to turn to the South upon the outbreak of war. As a young officer in the United States navy he invented a deep-sea sounding device used for surveying the North Pacific when the Civil War began. When Virginia entered the Confederacy, Brooke became one of Mallory's closest advisors. He strongly influenced the naval secretary in the early development of an ironclad program, and it was his design of a sea-going armored vessel that was adopted by Mallory and applied to the *Merrimack*. After the summer of 1862, however, Brooke lost interest in the ironclad program. Thenceforth he concerned himself primarily with matters of ordnance and hydrography.[21]

Brooke is best known for developing the standard gun used in the Confederate navy. The Brooke gun originated in the summer of 1861 when Mallory ordered the ordnance expert to design a seven-inch "rifle cannon" for the *Virginia*.[22] The guns were made of cast iron with a wrought iron rung shrunk onto the piece at the breech, in the manner perfected by the Northern foundryman, Robert P. Parrott, for his rifled field artillery. Where Parrott used only one band, Brooke doubled-banded and even triple-banded his breech rings.

The policy of contracting, whenever possible, for materials of war, was applied to ordnance and ordnance stores as well as to other war industries. Mallory reported to Congress that, "appreciating the importance of fostering private efforts to manufacture heavy guns for the Navy . . . a contract has been made with two establishments at New Orleans for casting . . . guns." Although the New Orleans venture was generally a failure, agreements with two private Richmond establishments, Tredegar Iron Works and Bellona Iron Works, were successful. The Bellona firm cast both smoothbores and rifles for the navy, but there is no record of their number or type. Tredegar was by far the most important facility for ordnance production in the Confederacy. Over 1,000 guns were cast during the war.[23]

In one instance the government bought out a private firm and engaged successfully in the manufacture of ordnance. In February 1862 a contract was signed between representatives of the War and Navy Departments and Colin J. McRae, a member of the naval affairs committee. McRae, with several other individuals, had recently purchased a foundry at Selma, Alabama, and he agreed to manufacture heavy ordnance and iron plates for gunboats. The contract stipulated that the first cannon should be cast by September 1 and the plates by the following December. McRae assumed the responsibility of placing the foundry in operation: he purchased machinery and tools, hired workmen, examined the rolling mills in Atlanta and Richmond, and contracted for iron ore and other materials, but the foundry was still inoperative when he was sent on a financial mission to Europe early in 1863. Before agreeing to accept this assignment, McRae made it a "condition of his acceptance" to be relieved of the Selma foundry "without pecuniary loss to himself." By the middle of February the Navy and War Departments had agreed to purchase and operate the foundry jointly, a venture which lasted only about three months since the Navy Department assumed complete control of the works on June 1, 1863.

When the navy took over, construction on the works had been under way for nearly sixteen months, but the first piece of ordnance was still to be produced. Under the capable supervision of Lieutenant Catesby ap R. Jones, the works were completed, and by the end of July the foundry was ready to cast its first gun. This gun, however, and those that immediately followed were experimental, and it was not until January 1864 that the first one was shipped for combat use. From then until the end of the war more than a hundred large naval guns were cast.

The bureau also organized facilities for the manufacture of ordnance stores (shell, shot, fuses, and caps): one at Norfolk and a second one at New Orleans. A congressional appropriation in April 1861 provided $30,000 for the Norfolk facility, which lasted less than a year. On March 26, 1862, Mallory sent a confidential dispatch to Captain Sidney Smith Lee, commander of the Norfolk navy yard, ordering him to prepare for possible evacuation. Tools and machinery not then in use were to be packed, ready for immediate shipment. On May 1 another dispatch to Lee directed that the transportation of the tools, machinery, and stores begin at once. No destination was named, but apparently a decision was made shortly afterward, for, on May 2, Lieutenant Robert D. Minor was ordered to Charlotte to locate and requisition suitable facilities for the Norfolk ordnance stores. This site was chosen not only because of its interior location but also because the city had excellent railroad connections with the coast. The department leased the Mecklenburg Iron Works for the new ordnance facility, and most of the machinery was installed there by the end of June. Within six months the establishment was in full operation, manufacturing gun carriages, shot, and other ordnance stores. The navy also shipped some of the Norfolk machinery and tools by way of the James

River to Richmond where an ordnance store and laboratory were placed in operation.

The department established an ordnance depot in Atlanta after New Orleans was threatened with capture and the ordnance facilities there had to be moved. In August 1861 Lieutenant Beverly C. Kennon had been assigned by the naval commandant in New Orleans to organize an ordnance store in the city. Within a month he had contracted for guns, gun carriages, projectiles, and powder; his expenditures amounted to nearly a million dollars. Unfortunately he exceeded his authority. As a result, many of his contracts were canceled, a large number of purchases returned, and Kennon himself transferred. Even so, it was some time before the naval office at New Orleans was out of debt. Kennon's replacement as ordnance officer, Lieutenant John R. Eggleston, was more conservative in his tenure, although he did establish a laboratory to manufacture primers and other ordnance parts. In the spring of 1862 Eggleston shipped the equipment in this laboratory and many of the stores gathered by Kennon to Atlanta. In Atlanta Lieutenant David P. McCorkle supervised the location of a new ordnance depot. The navy leased the property and buildings near the Georgia Railroad and installed machinery there. By the summer of 1862 these facilities were in operation.

The movement of ordnance depots inland, to Charlotte, Richmond, and Atlanta, was the last major organizational change in ordnance facilities during the war. On June 23, 1863, a circular from the ordnance bureau directed that "Hereafter, as far as practicable Ordnance Stores for the different naval stations will be supplied as follows: Richmond will supply Richmond and Wilmington; Charlotte will supply Charlotte, Savannah, Charleston; Atlanta will supply Mobile and the Gulf Stations."[24] This directive remained in effect until the end of the war, although Sherman's march to the sea resulted in the removal of the Atlanta facilities to North Carolina.

Powder was one material of war which the Confederate navy sadly lacked. The shortage of powder and of powder mills was severely felt at the beginning of the conflict. In fact, with the exception of 60,000 pounds captured at Norfolk, the navy had little power for its guns. The 1860 census shows only two small powder plants in the states which seceded: one in Tennessee employing ten men, the other in South Carolina employing three. Both the army and navy established new mills, although the only important naval powder factory was located at Petersburg, Virginia. Evidently, little if any powder was produced there before the mill was moved to Columbia, South Carolina, in August 1862. By 1864 this mill, under its civilian superintendent, P. Baudery Garésche, was manufacturing enough power to meet the navy's needs. Brooke reported early in 1865 that the mill was producing 20,000 pounds a month. The navy obtained its saltpeter principally from the Niter and Mining Bureau, but had agents in the field searching for this raw material.

On March 9, 1864, Grant was called from the West and appointed lieutenant general over all the armies of the Union. Grant planned his strategy for the destruction of the Confederate's two major armies: General William T. Sherman was to move from Chattanooga against Joseph E. Johnston's army, take Atlanta, and threaten the rear of Lee's army in Virginia. Grant himself was to conduct the Virginia campaign with the destruction of Lee's army as his objective. Subsidiary operations would include an advance up the James River from Fortress Monroe by a force under Butler and a campaign up the Red River in Louisiana by a combined naval and land force.

While Grant was grappling with Lee's army in Virginia, Sherman moved steadily through Georgia. After taking Atlanta, he cut his line of communication and began his epic march to the sea, taking Savannah in December 1864. From Savannah the Federal army turned north through South Carolina. In the face of Sherman's advance, the navy demolished one by one its facilities and destroyed its ships. Attempts were made to salvage equipment by moving to other localities, but generally this proved futile. As early as June 1864 the Atlanta Ordnance Works was evacuated, although the city was not threatened until August. The plant was then removed, first to Augusta, Georgia, and later to Fayetteville, North Carolina, where it was destroyed in February 1865. The Atlanta Rolling Mill was taken to Columbia, South Carolina, where it was gutted when the city burned. The naval squadrons, yards, and ships under construction in Savannah and Charleston were also put to the torch.

During the winter of 1865 while Sherman's army wreaked its vengeance upon the Carolinas, General James H. Wilson led a cavalry raid through Alabama and into Georgia. His objective was the destruction of Confederate stores, factories, mines, and ironworks in that area, including the naval establishments at Selma, Alabama, and Columbus, Georgia. On April 2, the day Richmond fell, Selma was occupied, and two weeks later the advance units of the Union cavalry reached Columbus. Catesby ap R. Jones at Selma lacked time to transfer his machinery. At Columbus Chief Engineer Warner sent a small vessel down the Chattahoochee to find a suitable site at which to relocate, but by the time the vessel returned it was too late. Naval facilities located in other cities—Mobile, Charlotte, Wilmington, and Richmond—were taken over or destroyed as Federal forces occupied the Confederacy.

The creation of facilities for building and for outfitting war vessels, despite the shortcomings of the program, was one of the most impressive accomplishments of the Confederate navy. At least twenty shipyards, five ordnance establishments, two marine machinery shops, a powder works, and a ropewalk were operated by or for the navy.[25] Undoubtedly Southern efforts to build a navy were hurt by the loss of New Orleans, Norfolk, and Pensacola in the spring of 1862. Military, geographic, and political reasons necessitated the dispersion of shipbuilding facilities. The Navy Department had to utilize small yards or develop new ones. Many of these yards were located on rivers, far enough upstream to protect them from Northern military operations. Charles Girard, a French correspondent who interviewed Mallory in 1863, wrote: "he has not been able to establish large naval construction yards for fear that they would fall into the hands of the enemy."[26] The availability of essential building materials was also a factor in locating yards. Mallory was unable to develop shipbuilding facilities in Texas and Arkansas because naval officers investigating the possibilities reported that adequate quantities of timber and iron were not available and could not be shipped in. Transportation was obviously essential and sites such as Atlanta and Columbus, Georgia; Shreveport, Louisiana; and Charlotte, North Carolina, were selected because of railroad connections. All of the Confederate states were threatened by amphibious attacks, and it was therefore necessary to develop naval defenses whenever possible. Admittedly Mallory made little effort to investigate individuals and firms who sought contracts for building war vessels. There were a number of cases in which he ordered naval officers to take over the supervision of completing a vessel when the work was apparently lagging; yet for political reasons he agreed to contract with individuals who had little or no experience in ship or boat building. John T. Shirley, the contractor for the two ironclads at Memphis, was not a shipbuilder, but he received a contract because of the strong recommendation of Representative David Currin of Memphis.

If Mallory could have concentrated naval construction in a few places such as Charleston, Savannah, Richmond, and one or two centers in the West, more vessels might have been completed, but this was impracticable under the circumstances. As it was, the facilities that were developed were handicapped by shortages of labor and deficiencies in certain materials, by inadequate transportation, and by the intense competition for the limited industrial facilities, workmen, and materials.

Materials

THE CONFEDERACY had, or developed, an adequate number of shipyards and related manufacturing establishments to build a navy. These facilities, however, were worthless without the raw materials, and the inability of the South to provide her industries with the essential raw materials, particularly iron, proved disastrous. As one authority has written, "The raw materials base of the Southern economy could not support the industrial superstructure, and this basic weakness contributed mightily to the ultimate collapse of the Confederate nation."[1]

In February 1864 General Benjamin Butler received a letter from one of his officers stating that it was only a "question of iron and time" before the ironclads under construction in North Carolina would be completed.[2] Although this officer was referring to only a few of the Confederate vessels, his statement was applicable to all. Probably the lack of iron and time contributed more to the failure of the Confederate shipbuilding program than anything else. Indeed, it is nearly impossible to exaggerate the effect of iron production on the entire Confederate war effort.

By 1860 the South, including Maryland and Kentucky, was producing approximately six-million-dollars worth of raw iron per year—nearly fourteeen per cent of the value of the total output in the United States. According to the 1860 census there were thirty-nine furnaces in the South producing 26,262 tons of pig iron: Tennessee had seventeen, Alabama four, Georgia two, and the remainder of the Confederate states had sixteen.[3] These figures, however, give no indication of the amount of ore that was available. With the exception of Florida, Louisiana, and Mississippi, all of the Confederate states had iron deposits ready to be mined, but the most important iron-producing section of the South—Kentucky, Tennessee, and western Virginia—fell into Union hands early in the war.[4] It then became necessary for the Confederacy to depend on the ore of the lower South, particularly that of northern Georgia and Alabama.

The failure of the Confederacy's railroads to provide adequate communication between the upper and lower South meant that Tredegar (the most important industry in the Confederate states) had to depend on the output of blast furnaces in Virginia. The vast Richmond works, capable of consuming annually between 20,000 and 24,000 long tons of pig iron, never had as much as 8,000 tons during any year year of the war.[5] The War and Navy Departments agreed by contract to supplement the blasts from Tredegar's own furnaces with enough iron to enable the works to meet their military production quotas. When the iron shortage brought the rolling of armor plate by Tredegar to a standstill in January 1863, the government promised to work out a system of priorities for the allocation of pig iron. This did not alleviate the situation, for as Dew states in his book: "The truth of the matter was that the government simply did not have the iron to give. . . ."[46]

The shortage of iron delayed the manufacture of guns, armor, and other equipment desperately needed by the navy to complete and outfit warships. Tredegar began rolling plates for the *Richmond* in April, but did not complete them until November 1862—almost twice as long as it took to roll the *Virginia's* armor. In December Tredegar's management wrote to the Navy Department: "We have considerable orders from two shops for bar iron, which cannot be executed for want of materials, and we can make no progress with the plate for Gun Boats for the same reason." In March 1863 Mallory complained of the slow delivery of armor and received a rather curt reply: "We cannot make more iron for want of the material. We have used every effort in our power to obtain it. . . ." On the last day of May 1863, a few days before the *Virginia II's* hull was launched, the president of Tredegar informed Mallory that the company was immediately having to "suspend the operation of making gun boat iron for want of material."[7] It would be nearly a year before this vessel was finally ready for action.

Between April 1861 and June 1863 the Office of Ordnance and Hydrography was responsible for obtaining the iron and other minerals required by the navy. This office contracted for 21,700 tons of iron within the first few months of the war, and by August 1862 it had added 107,500 tons (including 38,600 tons of plate iron). The navy also had an option on 37,356 tons for which the Ordnance Bureau of the army had written agreements. The contractors agreed to deliver the iron annually in varying stages (pigs, blooms, and plates) and in definite amounts.[8] There are no available records to indicate how much of this ore was delivered, although it is apparent that the amount must have been quite small.

In June 1863 the Secretary of War ordered the Niter and Mining Bureau to assume complete control over the mining of iron, copper, lead, coal, zinc, and "such other minerals as may be required for the prosecution of the war."[9] The War Department established this organization early in the war as a division of the Ordnance Bureau. It was organized originally for the purpose of obtaining saltpeter for making gunpowder, but the increasing importance of mining resulted in the bureau's becoming an independent body in April 1863. By the end of June it had undertaken the management of all mining activities, and its agents had final authority over the distribution of minerals. The navy's contracts were taken over, and until the end of the war the department was dependent upon this bureau for iron, copper, and other mineral ores. Nevertheless, it was quite clear that sufficient iron would not be obtained in this manner and that the navy would have to find other sources.

The government utilized three additional sources to acquire the iron needed for shipbuilding: importation, scrap iron, and railroad iron. Importation provided an undetermined amount of iron; most of it brought in through the blockade was in the nature of finish products, such as armor plates and machinery parts.[10] Scrap metal and particularly railroad iron proved to be of inestimable value to the navy in its shipbuilding program. In June 1862 Mallory wrote to one of his agents: "The want of Iron is pressing upon us and its supply is being curtailed. But one furnace is in blast in . . . Georgia, where there were formerly thirteen, and our agents are engaged in getting old iron from plantations and railroads. . . ."

The navy greatly desired railroad T-rails because they were easily rolled into strips of armor plate. The department first concentrated on acquiring unlaid rails and those from lines not in use. They obtained several hundred tons from the Atlantic and North Carolina Railroad, while a second line in North Carolina yielded over four thousand rails. In June 1862 naval agents confiscated 1,000 tons from the Albany and Gulf Company in southern Georgia, and in the following months purchased 3,000 tons from a small line in South Carolina. The small stock of rails not in use was soon exhausted, and the government began impressing iron from railroad companies owned by Northerners and from lines that were of little military value. In Georgia the Brunswick and Albany lost sixty miles of rails from Brunswick to Waynesville; in South Carolina the North Eastern reluctantly contributed iron to the navy for the vessels under construction at Charleston. The same was true of the Seaboard and Roanoke, the Petersburg and Weldon, and the Norfolk and Petersburg in Virginia; the Vicksburg, Shreveport, and Texas and the Southern Pacific in Louisiana and Texas. The city of Richmond even lost its horse car street tracks to the navy.[12]

The navy obtained many of the rails only after a great deal of trouble. Friction occurred throughout the war over the impressment of railroad iron. Not only the Navy Department but also the War Department, state governments, iron works, and railroad companies sent agents throughout the Confederacy laying claim to the rapidly-dwindling supply of railroad iron.

In April 1862 Mallory signed an order to seize the rails and fastenings of the Hungary branch of the Richmond, Fredericksburg, and Potomac line. The president of this road vainly complained that the railroad needed the iron more than any hypothetical fleet. In Georgia an agent of the department seized a quantity of rails belonging to the Atlantic and Gulf Railroad. This provoked Hiram Roberts, president of the A & G, who wrote to Mallory, President Davis, Secretary of War George W. Randolph, Beauregard, and General George Mercer (in command of the army in Savannah), demanding the return of the iron. When his demands were ignored, the leading citizens of Savannah drew up a petition requesting its release for the "local defense of this city." Mallory's continuous rejection resulted in Robert's refusal to ship the rails to the rolling mill in Atlanta over his road. This defiance was short-lived, for the Confederate government notified him that if he did not transport the iron the railroad would be seized. Repercussions continued for some time, however. The Navy Department dismissed the agent who originally stirred up the controversy by taking the iron, and turned his duties over to a navy officer. This officer was placed in a most awkward situation. He wrote to Catesby ap R. Jones shortly after assuming his new responsibilities: "Miner [the agent] has been taking the iron of the railroads for gun boat plates—promising to return it—there is nothing to return with and the railroads are down on us—in short a most frightful complicated box for a fellow to step in."[13]

In May 1863 Lieutenant George W. Gift, a Confederate naval officer at Columbus, Georgia, wrote Governor John Milton of Florida soliciting his aid in securing railroad iron for plating an ironclad under construction at Columbus. He pointed out to the governor that the completion of this vessel was just as vital to the interest of Florida as to Georgia. Milton evidently agreed, for two weeks later he replied that orders had been given to turn over to the navy rails belonging to the Florida Railroad Company. Unfortunately, strong opposition developed from General Joseph Finegan, Confederate commander in East Florida, who considered the road indispensable for the defense of his district, and David L. Yulee, one of Florida's senators in the Confederate Congress. Although the principal stockholders in the company were New Yorkers, Yulee was also a stockholder and the president. For over a year a controversy raged between the senator and the railroad company on the one hand and Milton and the Confederate Government on the other. In spite of a court injunction part of the road was finally dismantled late in 1863, the government used some of the rails to construct a line from Lake City, Florida, to the Georgia border and shipped an undetermined number to Atlanta to be rolled into plate.[14] The *Jackson*, the vessel under construction at Columbus, eventually received her armor, but she was completed just in time to be destroyed when the city was captured in the Spring of 1865.

In Charleston, Beauregard, angry with the navy for refusing to turn over iron for a torpedo boat which one of his officers was building, attempted to manipulate political support to gain the armor. The general asked Senator William P. Miles of South Carolina and Governor Milledge L. Bonham to use their influence to have railroad iron designated for ironclads being built in Charleston transferred to the torpedo boat. Miles wrote the secretary of war that the army vessel would be worth two gunboats, but efforts on the part of both the secretary and Miles to gain Mallory's approval were fruitless. Beauregard asked Bonham to apply pressure on the navy by threatening to transfer mechanics at work on one of the state gunboats under construction if the iron was not released, but the governor refused to be drawn into the controversy.[15] Consequently the "torpedo ram" was never armored.

The navy's search for railroad iron was a long and frus-

ONE HUNDRED HANDS WANTED,

AT THE

CONFEDERATE
STATES NAVY YARD!

LOCATED ON THE

CHATTAHOOCHEE RIVER!

AT

Saffold, Early Co., Georgia.
To Build Gun Boats!

SHIP Carpenters, Joiners, Caulkers, Mechanics of every kind, Blacksmiths, Hewers and Laborers, both white men & negroes, can find employment at the Confederate States Navy Yard. As several Gun Boats are now in progress of construction and under contract, the hands may expect steady employment and good wages.

All the hands employed at the Navy Yard are exempt from Military duty, and not subject to a draft.

Any person now in the service, who desires a situation at the Navy Yard, can obtain a Furlough to work there, by application to D. S. Johnston. Saffold, Early county, Ga.

The Confederate States Navy Yard is situated on the Chattahoochee River, at Saffold, Early county, Ga., and is accessible by Steamboats making regular trips from Columbus, Ga., via Eufaula, Ala., and Fort Gaines, Ga.

D. S. JOHNSTON.

Saffold, Ga., Mar. 5, 1862. 20-tf

A call for workmen by the Saffold, Georgia, Navy Yard. The inability to secure adequate, skilled labor was to plague the Confederate Navy throughout the war. (Courtesy of Confederate Naval Museum)

The Confederate Navy Yard at Columbus, Georgia, was typical of the many inland construction sites established after the first year of the war. This facility constructed the ironclad *Jackson* ("*Muscogee*") and torpedo boat *Viper*, and repaired the gunboat *Chattaboochee* after her accidental sinking in 1863. (Courtesy of Confederate Naval Museum)

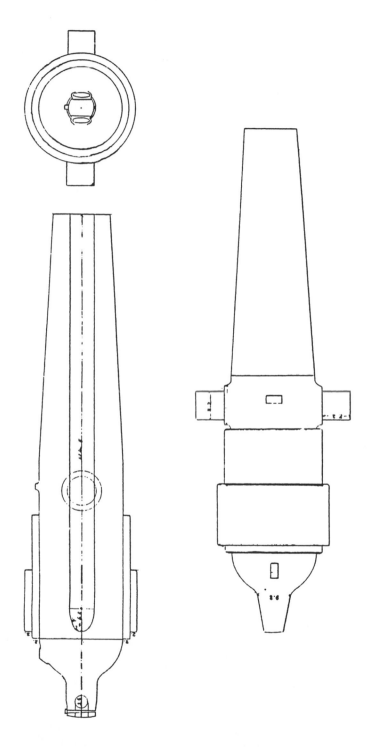

The development and production of the Brooke naval cannon was one of the greatest feats of the Confederate Navy. Produced in several calibers, both rifled and smoothbore, the Brooke became the South's standard shipboard gun. (Courtesy of National Archives)

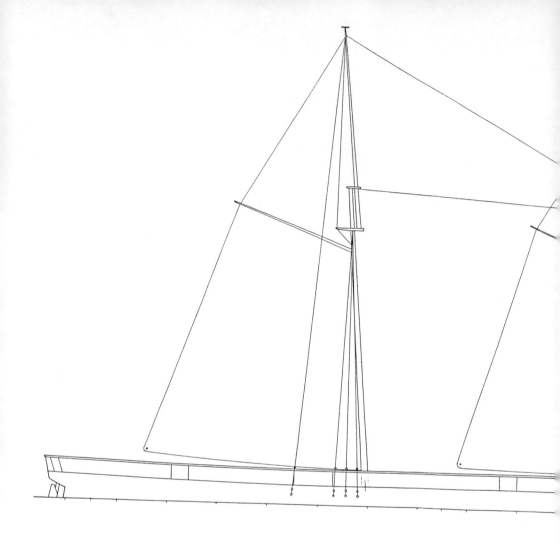

Berth Deck and Magazine
Wooden Gun Boat 150 ft. lg. 25 ft. bm.
10 ft. depth.

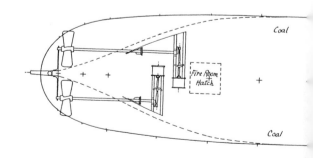

Coal

Fire Room
Hatch

Coal

These drawings of the C.S.S. *Macon*, a spar plan and berth deck plan, represent the only extant builder's plans of any of the early-war Confederate wooden gunboats. (Redrawn by Robert Holcombe from original plans held by Special Collections, Robert W. Woodruff Library, Emory University.)

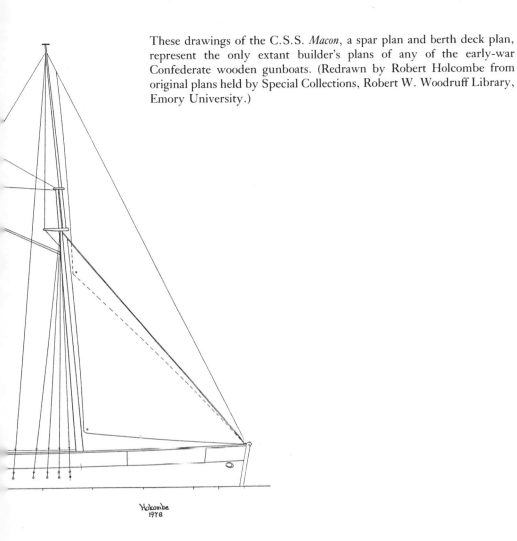

Holcombe
1978

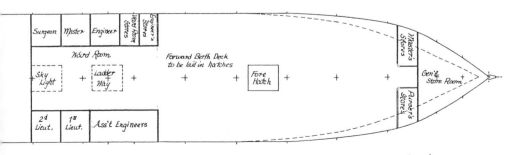

Holcombe
1977

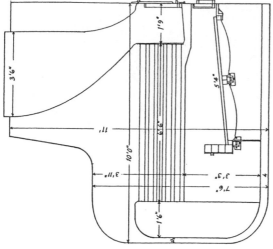
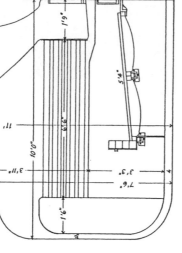

Holcombe '78

This pair of low-pressure, fire tube boilers was produced by the C.S. Naval Iron Works, Columbus, Georgia. Commanded by Chief Engineer James H. Warner, this facility became the most important in the Confederacy for the construction of marine steam machinery. (Redrawn by Robert Holcombe from the original in the James H. Warner Collection, Confederate Naval Museum.)

Fewer than half of the warships laid down in the South ever reached an operational status. Many, including this ironclad at Krenson and Hawkes shipyard in Savannah, were destroyed by the Confederates to prevent capture by advancing union forces. (Courtesy of Robert Holcombe)

A voucher for payment to Scofield and Markham Rolling Mill for the rolling of armor plate for the ironclads *Huntsville* and *Tuscaloosa*. (Courtesy of National Archives) trating affair in North Carolina. In October 1862 the War Department turned down Mallory's request for a quantity of rails belonging to the Portsmouth and Weldon road. The naval secretary then heard of a considerable amount of iron belonging to the Atlantic and North Carolina Railroad Company of which the principal stockholder was the state of North Carolina. He immediately wrote to Governor Zebulon Vance for permission to take the rails. Vance agreed, but news of this reached other stockholders, whose protests resulted in the withdrawal of the governor's consent. At the same time, however, he suggested that the rails belonging to the Seaboard and Roanoke line (Northern-owned) be confiscated. The navy obtained these rails, but by the beginning of 1863 there was still not enough iron available to armor even one of the four ironclads under construction in North Carolina.

In January 1863 Mallory received a letter from one of his officers in charge of the construction of ironclads in North Carolina:

> It is impossible to obtain any Rail Road iron unless it is seized. The Petersburg Rail Road agent says that he must have the old iron on the Petersburg to replace the worn out rails on that road. The Kinston and Raleigh Road require the iron taken below Kinston to replace the iron on the Charlotte & North Carolina Road and those Roads are considered a military necessity and the whole subject of Railroad iron was laid before the North Carolina Legislature and I am unable to obtain iron.[16]

He then recommended to Mallory that "if no iron can be obtained to clad these boats, I think the entire work ought to be abandoned." The secretary forwarded a copy of this letter to Vance with the notation that "the vessels would not have been undertaken had the Department not had good reason to believe the Rail Road iron could be obtained in North Carolina." Mallory's prodding was somewhat successful, for the governor was able to persuade a reluctant railroad company to part with a large number of rails. By the summer of 1863 the navy had acquired over 2,000 tons of iron, but it would be nearly a year before the metal could be rolled into plate and transported back to the building sites.[17]

On January 22, 1863, the Adjutant and Inspector General's Office announced the creation of a "commission to examine and advise on what railroad in the Confederate States the iron on their tracks can be best be dispensed with."[18] This was the result of a directive from Davis ordering the secretaries of war and navy to work out some plan for taking up railroad iron. The order creating the commission also stipulated that the use of impressed rails was specifically limited to the construction of vessels-of-war and the building of railroad connections designated by Congress as necessary to military operations. This commission was able to eliminate much of the competition, but the inadequate supply of iron prevented a solution to the railroad iron problem. In January 1864 the chief of the army's Engineer Bureau wrote the secretary of war that "no iron-clads have effected any good, nor are likely to effect any"; he then recommended that all "naval iron" be turned over to the army for railroad use.[19]

The mad scramble for railroad iron certainly points out the dilemma which the Confederacy faced. Which should have priority—the plating of warships, or the replacing of worn-out rails on the various railroads? This dilemma was never solved: many of the ships never received their armor, and the railroads continued to deteriorate throughout the war. In both cases the results were disastrous to the Confederate war effort.

Railroad iron was only a small part of the metal problem that faced the Confederacy. The government realized that the only solution was to increase the amount of iron mined and produced. Early in 1862 both the secretary of war and the secretary of the navy began urging Davis that additional government action was needed to assure a supply of pig iron for the Confederate war efforts. On March 12 Secretary Judah P. Benjamin warned Davis that "The supply of iron . . . will soon be far short of our wants both for cannon and for the construction of gunboats."[20] Nine days later Mallory notified the President that Tredegar was unable to meet its production quotas and to deliver promised cannon, munitions, and armor plate because of pig iron shortages. Shortly after this he wrote to Albert Gallatin Brown, chairman of the Senate Naval Affairs Committee, and urged the adoption of a policy of making advance payments to individuals and firms for the purpose of stimulating the production of iron and coal.[21] The War Department already had approval to pursue such a procedure, and Congress hastily followed suit for the navy. On April 19, a week after Brown received Mallory's request, Congress passed a bill authorizing the government to lend up to fifty per cent of the capital needed to erect or expand "all establishments or mines for the production of coal and for the production and manufacture of iron." This bill not only gave the Navy Department the authorization it wanted, but also liberalized the law that the War Department already followed.[22]

Between 1862 and 1865 thirteen new blast furnaces were built in Alabama, and fifteen in Virginia, the two most important iron-producing states in the Confederacy. The government advanced most of the necessary funds for their development. The furnaces, like other manufacturing facilities in the Confederacy, were required to furnish definite percentages of their output to the war effort, a policy of production control that resulted in a great deal of dissatisfaction to the contractors and producers. The Confederate government purchased the Bibb Iron Company in Alabama, because the owners refused to comply with governmental regulations regarding output. Most iron works, however, seem to have been kept in line by controlling their labor supply and transportation.

In spite of the new furnaces the amount of iron produced was not substantially increased. The reason was the gradual occupation of the Confederacy by Union forces. By October 1864 ten large furnaces in Virginia, all but three in Tennessee, all in Georgia, and all but four in Alabama had been burned out or lost to Federal troops.[23] These losses offset the new furnaces that were built. Although Alabama was producing four times as much raw iron as any other state, by the end of 1864 the total output was still rather meager. In November Congress set up a committee to examine the crucial iron situation, but it could suggest nothing new. Little could be done, for time was not available; the iron was in the mines, and there most of it remained through the war.[24]

Other metals that shipbuilders used in naval construction included zinc, copper, and tin. Of these only copper was available within the Confederacy; the others had to be brought in through the blockade. In January 1865 Brooke reported to Mallory: "For cast steel, copper, tin and zinc, we are dependent on foreign countries. . . . Fortunately, we have received from abroad, chiefly through Wilmington, . . . a supply sufficient for several months."[25] Brooke however, was referring to ordnance production; copper remained so scarce throughout the war that few Confederate vessels had their bottoms sheathed. At least one ironclad, the *North Carolina*, was lost because of this deficiency.[26] The government obtained some copper during the early months of the war from East Tennessee, but in 1862 the area where these mines were located was overrun by Union forces.

Although the South, with the exception of the trans-Mississippi West, had an abundant supply of coal in its mines, naval squadrons and facilities were continually short of this fuel. During the month of July 1863 the naval stations at Charleston, Savannah, and Columbus had 170 tons of coal to divide among them. At one time vessels in the Charleston squadron received fifteen tons a day. In January 1864 the squadron's commander had to inform Beauregard, commander of the military department that included Charleston, that his ironclads could no longer patrol nightly between Forts Moultrie and Sumter because of the lack of coal.[27]

There were a number of quarrels over coal. Governor Vance and the Navy Department became involved in a bitter controversy over some coal which the army commandeered at Wilmington, and in the Trans-Mississippi Department the meager supply of coal resulted in a number of serious disputes between army and navy officers.[28]

Transportation was, as usual, the basic cause of the coal shortage. One of the naval officers in charge of coal distribution wrote: "The principal difficulty in securing coal now arises, not from its scarcity, for there is an abundance of it at the mines, but from the limited means of transportation. . . ."[29] The navy possessed only forty-five coal cars to carry coal to the Charleston, Savannah, and Columbus facilities, while the absence of railroad transportation between the coal mines in central Alabama and Mobile resulted in the building of a number of coal barges.

The responsibility for supplying coal to the navy was frequently shifted during the war; in fact, the department never rendered a clear-cut decision as to where it should rest. At first the Office of Provisions and Clothing assumed this duty, but its attempts to contract for coal were completely unsuccessful. Agreements were made with Robert Jemison, Jr., of Tuscaloosa, Alabama, and James Browne of Charleston, South Carolina, for 25,000 tons of coal, but none of this was delivered. Confederates confiscated a large supply at New Orleans and Norfolk, and divided it among the various naval stations.[30] At the same time station and facility commanders contracted for coal, a procedure not authorized but practiced throughout the war. In September 1862 the department transferred the responsibility for coal to the Office of Orders and Detail, and Commander John K. Mitchell was appointed superintendent of "coal contracts."[31] Then in June 1863 the government extended the control of the Niter and Mining Bureau to include coal. Until the end of the war, in theory, this bureau supplied all coal to the navy as well as to the army; however, it was apparent that the bureau's control was rather loose, for the navy continued to obtain coal on its own. For example, the Office of Ordnance and Hydrography throughout the war contracted for coal for its various ordnance facilities. The situation became further confused when the Office of Orders and Details designated an ordnance officer, Catesby ap R. Jones, "to take charge of the Coal contracts of the Department and organize it. . . ."[32]

Jones may have been responsible for the organization of the distribution of coal that was inaugurated by the navy in October 1864. The naval stations at Richmond and Wilmington and the naval works at Charlotte received their coal from the mines in the vicinity of Richmond. Charleston and Savannah obtained coal from the Egypt mines in the Deep River Basin of North Carolina; the Mobile Station, as well as the naval establishments at Columbus and Augusta, Georgia, drew on the mines near Montevallo, Alabama.[33] There is no evidence that this reorganization alleviated the coal shortage.

Studies of the Civil War that point out the inadequate economic resources of the Confederacy have failed to emphasize one material which was vitally important to the navy—timber. Perhaps this is because the South has always abounded in forests, and the timber industry was important even before the war. Nevertheless, seasoned timber was scarce in 1861; the result was that most of the ships constructed in the Confederacy were built of green timber.

Only a few of the five-hundred or more species of trees found in North America have been used in shipbuilding. White and live oak were, prior to the war, the primary timbers used in the frames of American ships. White oak, characterized by its lightness, was more important because of its accessibility to the shipyards along the northeastern coast of the United States, but builders considered live oak to be stronger and more durable. In the years prior to the war shipbuilders were using more live oak, particularly in naval construction. Live oak, found primarily in the Southern states, was the most important timber used by the Confederate navy in shipbuilding. Southern builders also used longleaf pine for planking, decking, and in the construction of cabins. There was no shortage of this timber in the Southern states.[4]

There were small quantities of seasoned timber scattered throughout the Confederacy when the war began, but far from enough for an extensive shipbuilding program. The South obtained a large supply when the Gosport Navy Yard was seized, but most of this was burned when Norfolk was recaptured by Federal forces in 1862. Mallory frequently urged his officers to be on the lookout for seasoned timber and to impress it for the department when located. Very little, however, was acquired in this manner. He was also interested in building up the reserves of shipbuilding timber, and in April 1861 he wrote in his report to the president: "The preservation of forest timber for naval shipbuilding requires the attention of Congress . . . and while Great Britain, France, and Russia are carefully guarding and providing for the preservation of every forest tree of their own useful for naval purpose . . . we can not with prudence ignore the subject. . . ."[35] Timber reserves would not be established during the few years that the Confederacy existed.

Naval construction was seriously handicapped by the shortage of seasoned timber. Green timber had to be used extensively, and this resulted in ships that leaked and constantly needed repair. When the *Louisiana* was launched water poured into her gundeck, and she nearly swamped. One of the reasons that the *Albermarle* was anchored as a battery with a protective log boom around her was that she leaked badly. Upon the cessation of hostilities the United States Navy Department condemned the various Confederate vessels that fell into its hands. Surveys made of the *Missouri, Nashville, Tennessee,* and others all indicated that they were unseaworthy because of green timber used in their construction. If the Confederacy's bid for independence had been successful, the navy would have had to rebuild its ships because of the use of green timber during the war.

The Confederacy potentially had the necessary raw materials as well as facilities for shipbuilding. The problem was the transmutation of the materials from their raw state into finished products, and, later, the assembly of these finished products into a vessel-of-war and its equipage. What was needed was labor and, above all, time.

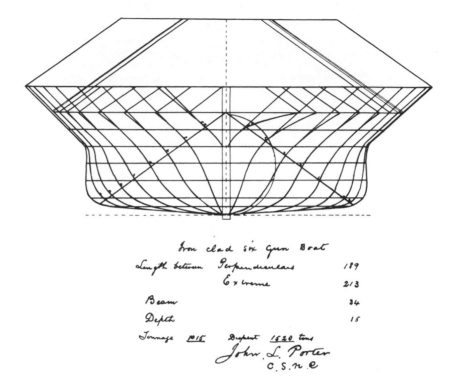

Iron clad six gun Boat
Length between Perpendiculars   189
            Extreme   213
Beam   34
Depth   15
Tonnage 1015   Displacmt 1520 tons
                    John L. Porter
                       C.S.n.e

Ironclad ram. Fourth of the ironclads to be built for the Confederate Government at Charleston, S. C. Contract for hull awarded to F. M. Imes, that for plating and machinery to I. M. Eason. Built of white oak and yellow pine. Casemate covered with of 1 inch iron. Originally plated with three thicknesses of 2 inch iron, one on and two ready to be put on. Launched shortly before the evacuation of Charleston, February 18, 1865. A Confederate account states that she was so much injured by running aground "as not to be of any service whatever."

Admiral Dahlgren reports: "The rebel ram Columbia which was all ready for service, armed, manned, steam up—had grounded coming out of the dock January 12, 1865 was saved by us after much effort and was floated April 26. Pierced for 6 guns—one at each side, one at each of the four corners—pivots to point ahead or stern and to the side. Two engines, high pressure. Plated on casemate with 6-inch of iron in thickness; quite equal to the best of the kind built by the rebels."

In ordinary Navy Yard, Norfolk, Va. 1866, 1867.

Labor

IF THE Confederacy had been fortunate enough to have had an abundance of the necessary materials for shipbuilding, the shortage of labor, both skilled and unskilled, would still have severely curtailed construction. Throughout the war agriculture, transportation, and industry were constantly struggling with the military for the rapidly decreasing labor supply. Probably the South had a sufficient number of artisans at the beginning of the war to provide a basic force, but within a few months industries were suffering because of a short supply of workers. According to the 1860 census there were 570 ship and boat carpenters and mechanics and 4,570 workers in machinery works in the Southern states. Many industries, however, had depended on aliens for much of their labor, and an exodus of foreigners and Northerners began shortly after Fort Sumter. Also over-mobilization at the beginning of the conflict swept most of the skilled workers into the army.

The Navy Department was not pressed for labor throughout 1861, for most ship construction carried out was in locations which had an adequate labor.[1] Nevertheless, Mallory was already concerned about obtaining an adequate supply of skilled workmen. The navy's needs for mechanics and carpenters increased as shipbuilding expanded, and as the ordnance works and other facilities began operating.[2]

In August 1861 the naval secretary began a long and frustrating correspondence with the War Department concerning shipwrights and mechanics in the army. He requested that ship carpenters, "as may be willing to receive discharge . . . ," be released to work for the navy.[3] The secretary of war ordered commanding officers to discharge these men, but from the beginning opposition developed. John T. Shirley, a shipbuilder at Memphis under contract to the navy, sent a list of thirty or more carpenters and their regiments to General Leonidas Polk with the request that they be released for naval service. Polk denied the request. Shirley then asked the general to furnish a detail of one-hundred men to work on two ironclads under construction—eight appeared. Similar occurrences took place throughout the Confederacy. This opposition from Polk and other army officers to detailing men for naval construction resulted in the secretary of war's modifying his original order. In December the secretary of war notified Mallory that all requests for mechanics and carpenters would be refused unless "the parties interested will furnish substitutes."[4] That is, the navy had to provide a replacement for any soldier obtained from the army.

The refusal of the War Department to provide workmen unless they were replaced by substitutes prompted Mallory in January 1862 to urge the president to take action to secure from the army the services of carpenters, shipwrights, and joiners who would volunteer to work on the construction of ships for the navy. In response to this appeal Davis wrote to the secretary of war: "As far as practicable it will be proper to aid in the work, but it must be considered that no effort is to be spared to find mechanics elsewhere than in the army."[5] Unfortunately, there were few other sources, and subsequent appeals to Davis were virtually ignored. The naval secretary wrote rather bitterly in his diary that "the President refused to permit a man to leave the army to work on gunboats."[6]

Congressional action was also tried, but there the matter became involved in conscription legislation. On March 20, 1862, a bill entitled "an act to provide for ascertaining and detailing artizans and mechanics from the Confederate Army" was passed by the Senate and sent to the House. But there the bill was delayed and finally killed when Davis on March 29 asked for the conscription of all men between the ages of eighteen and thirty-five. Six months later a second conscription act extended the upper military age from thirty-five to forty-five. This first selective service program in American history also included exemptions from military service. On April 21 Congress passed the first exemption law which established the system of exempting various classes of persons. This law was repealed in October 1862 and a more detailed one was enacted. These laws apparently worked quite well for a time in protecting the labor already employed in the manufacturing facilities (including naval), but the core of the matter as far as labor was concerned was still unsolved— namely the acquisition of workers from the army. No provisions were included for releasing or transferring carpenters and mechanics to work for the navy, and no legislation pertaining to this matter passed Congress.[7]

In January the War Department began the policy of detailing men from the army to work on ships and in various naval establishments. The system was gradually expanded to include all types of manufacturing in the Confederacy. President Davis preferred this to exemptions because full control could be retained over men assigned, but until 1864 he was unable to get this into law. The absence of legislative authority ostensibly had little effect, for the detailing of men was used extensively from 1862 until the end of the war. The War Department apparently cooperated fully in this system, but there was one factor which ruined its effectiveness—the allocation of men was left to the discretion of commanding officers of various units. This applied to all levels from generals in command of armies to company commanders.

By the spring of 1862 military commanders were faced with an increasingly-serious manpower shortage. Volunteering brought thousands to the colors during the first months of the war, but this impulse began to fade early in 1862. After the reversals suffered in the fall and winter of 1861-1862, the people awakened to the fact that the war was no longer a picnic. It was hoped that the conscription law passed in the spring of 1862 would encourage volunteering (most Southerners regarded being drafted as a disgrace), but it probably hurt more than it helped. The law granted the right to avoid military service by sending a substitute, and provided for a large number of exemptions, including ministers, college professors, druggists, postmasters, employees of railroads, ferrymen, printers, tanners, saltmakers, employees in cotton and woolen mills, mines, furnaces, and foundries. The measure was also strongly resented by many state governors, a large segment of the public, and soldiers in the ranks. Hundreds of men expressed their resentment by deserting. Under these circumstances it is understandable that army officers resented efforts to deplete their units for industrial work.

On December 10, 1862, the secretary of war denied a request from Mallory for ship carpenters. He justified his refusal on the grounds that his commanders in the field and military districts were almost unanimously opposed to providing men for naval work. Many (perhaps most) army officers agreed with General George E. Pickett who said that not only should all such requests be refused but that every man already detailed should be ordered back to his unit.[8]

Lieutenant Jonathan H. Carter, trying to complete the ironclad *Missouri* at Shreveport, Louisiana, complained that with few exceptions military officers refused to detail men to work on the vessel. In February 1863 Admiral Franklin Buchanan, in command of the Mobile Station, applied for carpenters, but was turned down because "the Commanders of armies from which these details are requested report that they can not spare the men. . . ."[9]

Contractors encountered similar opposition and red tape. On September 10, 1862, Colin J. McRae, under contract to establish an ordnance works and rolling mill at Selma, Alabama, wrote the chief of the Bureau of Ordnance and Hydrography:

> When I made the contract with the Secretaries of War and Navy it was understood between you, Colonel Gorgas & myself that the Departments were to give me all the

aid they could in procuring both materials and mechanics. Though I have applied for the detail of a good many mechanics from the army I have never succeeded in getting but one and now a cancellation of his detachment by the army has deprived me of his services. . . .[10]

A shipbuilder at Yazoo City, Mississippi, trying in various ways to persuade the army to provide carpenters, caulkers, and mechanics, sent letters and telegrams as well as agents to military commands in Mississippi and Alabama; but none were obtained except a few provided by General John C. Pemberton at Vicksburg.[11]

The naval ordnance facilities evidently had even more difficulty in acquiring mechanics from the army. In the spring of 1864 Brooke, chief of the Office of Ordnance and Hydrography, wrote to his subordinates commanding ordnance works requesting them to study their labor needs and report in detail to him. The replies clearly illustrate the problems and effects of the policy of details. Chief Engineer Henry A. Ramsey of the Charlotte establishment reported that "a number of our more important tools are idle a large portion of the time for the want of mechanics to work them . . . and many of the large forgings required in the building and arming of war vessels can only be made with the assistance of these tools. . . ." McCorkle's report from Atlanta was even more dismal:

At one time last year I had no lumber for shell boxes and the commander of the camp of instruction in this district refused to detail a sawyer who owned a mill on the ground that the man wished to get out of the Army by obtaining a contract. . . . I have been four months unable to have forged the wrought iron bolts for the Brooke gun for the want of blacksmiths. Major General Maury detailed a second rate blacksmith to me, but revoked the order two weeks ago. . . . I have asked for details until I am tired; and even those conscripts who are unwillingly detailed to the works are accompanied by so many orders and so many papers (the orders are changed once a week) that a clerk is constantly employed to try and keep their papers correct.

> It would appear that officers employed in manufacturing
> ordnance are not deemed patriotic by the Conscript Bureau
> as they seem to think that an officer who asks for the de-
> tail of a man to do Government work is doing something
> wrong. . . .[12]

McCorkle's disgust over the red tape required to obtain
and retain details led him to ignore orders to return men to
their units, but a threat from the secretary of war to with-
draw all details from the Atlanta works brought him in line.

McCorkle was not the only one who tried to evade the
correct procedure for acquiring mechanics. It became quite
common for naval officers and contractors to hire soldiers
who were home on leave and then to request their services
from the army. In some cases where naval officers or builders
hired the workers without notifying their units, the employers
assumed the responsibility of protecting the "deserter" (as he
was officially) from the provost marshal.[13]

After the conscription law of February 1864 went into
effect, the retention of details became even more difficult.
The enrolling officers had the authority to grant details
for only sixty days at a time, and at the end of the stipulated
period the contractor or naval officer had to make a new
application. In a majority of cases the War Department ordered the details returned to their units despite protests from
the navy. The situation became so intolerable that in April
1864 Mallory wrote to the president:

> A perpetual struggle exists between the military officers
> from whose commands these mechanics are detailed and
> the naval officers under whom they are employed for
> their possession. The Navy Department received almost
> daily notices of the revocation of the details of its work-
> men, or of calls for their return to their command, while
> the mechanic himself uncertain as to what moment he may
> be returned to a marching regiment is discontented and
> neglects means and opportunities for improving his con-
> dition. . . .[14]

He then recommended once again that mechanics be transferred (rather than detailed) to the navy, and suggested that these men be required to enlist in the navy. The naval secretary added, "While this would lead to the improvement of the condition of the individual artisan, it would at the same time by placing a body of men permanently under the distinct organization and discipline of the Navy . . . render them more efficient. . . ."[15] Actually Brooke and other naval officers had advocated this plan for some time as the logical solution to the labor problem. McCorkle had further recommended that if the workers "misbehave, send them on board ship. . . ."

Under existing circumstances the plan would possibly have alleviated the labor problem if time permitted. In December 1864 a bill incorporating this plan was introduced in the House of Representatives, but the war was over before it passed into law.

Conscription interfered seriously with the navy's shipbuilding program in an additional way. A large number of the skilled laborers were foreigners and Northerners who remained in the Confederacy primarily because of the relatively high wages. The introduction of conscription and the tightening of exemption policies resulted in an increasing exodus from manufacturing facilities.[16] The War Department organized a Bureau of Conscription to administer the draft and either enroll or exempt all eligible males. The army established conscript camps in various parts of the Confederacy, and naval officers and agents made frequent trips to these camps seeking workers. On October 10, 1863, the War Department forwarded a circular to all conscript camps directing the enrolling officers to "respect the certificates of agents authorized by the Secretary of the Navy, given to persons engaged in the construction of ships, gunboats, engines. . . ." More often than not, however, recruiters sent to obtain men for naval work were given the "run around" by enrolling officers. Naval officers found it difficult to persuade conscript camp officials to consign men for shipbuilding and ordnance work.

By the winter of 1863-1864, the desperate need for additional soldiers led Congress, on February 17, to pass a new conscription act. This act drafted for the duration all white men between the ages of seventeen and fifty, although the boys of seventeen and the men between forty-five and fifty were to be employed as reserves in their home states. This act also repealed all industrial exemptions. The President obtained by this law the authority to detail men as he saw fit for industrial work. To the navy this new law simply compounded its labor problems. Now the naval secretary must go directly to President Davis, and to Davis, the manpower need in the army had reached such proportions that it appeared to overshadow everything else. The navy obtained few additional workers from conscript camps after February 1864 and had to develop other means to fill its labor needs.

From the beginning the navy had made efforts to relieve its labor shortage in various ways. One was to import artisans from the North and abroad. The Confederate government, while still meeting in Montgomery, Alabama, ordered Raphael Semmes north to hire mechanics, but the few that were persuaded to come south left with the outset of hostilities.[17] The government ordered Commander James D. Bulloch and other agents in Europe to employ skilled workers and arrange for their transportation to the Confederacy. They offered inducements such as high wages, exemption from military service, and constant employment, but few were persuaded to attempt the risky passage through the blockade. Some did come to the Confederate states, but their stay was usually quite short: the wartime conditions in the South, constant threat of invasion and occupation by Union forces, and the hostility of Southerners because of special privileges resulted in most of them leaving after a few months.[18] The government also paroled an undetermined number of Northern prisoners-of-war who were skilled workers to work in Confederate war industries, but there is no evidence that any of them were employed in naval facilities.[19]

The national government also contacted the governors of the different states in order to secure the services of skilled workers in state military units. Governor John J. Pettus of

Mississippi received a number of letters from shipbuilders requesting him to detail ship carpenters and caulkers in state units to work on vessels under construction at Yazoo City.[20] Similar appeals were made to governors Vance of North Carolina, John G. Shorter of Alabama, and Joseph E. Brown of Georgia, but there is no information to indicate whether or not they complied with the requests.

The Navy Department followed other methods to relieve the labor situation in its shipyards and ordnance facilities including night shifts, Sunday work, and overtime whenever possible. The policy of shifting skilled labor from facility to facility, particularly shipyards, in order to expedite construction became standard practice. This applied to specialists such as constructors and master carpenters.[21]

The navy used Negro labor extensively, both skilled and unskilled, in its many establishments. At first slave labor was usually hired from local planters to cut timber, work the mines, and perform other tasks requiring unskilled labor, but the use of Negroes as skilled workers increased throughout the war. Although slaves were not used widely in manufacturing before the war, Negroes, usually free, were skilled in many trades. For example, a majority of the ship carpenters in Charleston were Negro.[22] The exact number of Negroes the government employed in naval establishments is impossible to determine, but in February 1865 Brooke reported to Mallory that the ordnance establishments under his control were using approximately half Negro labor (541 Negro and 532 white).[23]

Probably the worst aspect of the labor problem was the bitter rivalry that developed over the procurement and retention of skilled workmen. This competition involved rivalries between the military authorities and private industry, between army and navy, and even intra-service rivalries. As early as September 1862 McRae, the organizer of the naval ordnance works at Selma, Alabama, wrote to the Navy Department accusing Commander Farrand, in charge of the Selma shipyard, of luring foundry mechanics to the shipyard by offering higher wages. He added, "so far from securing assistance from the Department in completing my works, its officers are embarrassing me. . . ."[24] Even after the navy assumed control of the works, competition between it and the shipyard continued. In December 1862 the management of Tredegar complained to Mallory: "Our operations for your Department are now being interfered with to such an extent by the efforts of establishments being built elsewhere, especially at Selma, to draw off our hands that we beg to invoke your prompt and serious attention to the subject."[25]

This tug-of-war over labor was even more serious between the two branches of the service, particularly in cities where both army and navy establishments were located. The commanding officer of the arsenal at Selma wrote to the secretary of war complaining of the competition between that depot and the naval facilities of the city. Similar complaints from other army installations resulted in a recommendation by the secretary that "consultations between the officers of the respective Departments commanding establishments at the same posts" would perhaps alleviate the situation.[26] This suggestion was never put into practice, however, and the dissension over labor continued to the end.

The basis for this trouble was the wage scale, a problem aggravated because of the rapidly-depreciating value of Confederate money. Wages were continually rising, and when one facility in a particular locality raised its wage scale, all other establishments locally would either have to follow suit or lose their labor. To complicate matters further, the policy of detailing men to industries created dissension between civilian employees and the detailed men who received only their army pay. In January 1864 Congress finally passed a law providing for compensation to army personnel detached to work in war industries.[27]

Financing the war was the most difficult task confronting the Confederate government. There was very little hard money in the South when the war began, and the government turned first to loans as a means of securing funds, and later to the issuing of treasury notes. Neither scheme was completely successful, but the second one at least provided the government with the means of meeting its mounting debts. Nevertheless, during the first year and a half, even treasury notes were scarce and bonds had to be used to take care of government expenditures, including shipbuilding.[28]

Unquestionably the financial situation seriously affected naval construction. Throughout the war the navy placed second to the army in Congressional appropriations. In order to obtain funds for naval expenditures, Mallory followed the procedure of requisitioning the Treasury Department for specific sums authorized by law. When the naval secretary was notified that the requisition had been approved, paymasters were given the authority to draw on government depositories. The navy, however, found it continually difficult to obtain funds; the secretary of the treasury was frequently slow in approving requisitions from the Navy Department; depositories were often unable to provide naval paymasters with the necessary amounts in treasury notes. In February 1862 Mallory wrote to the secretary of the treasury that "the operations of this Department are much endangered and the credit of the government damaged by the delays incurred in placing funds in New Orleans to meet expenditures. . . ."[29] In March the paymaster in New Orleans telegraphed the naval secretary that funds were still not available to pay off debts incurred in January. The situation became so embarrassing that the "Committee of Public Safety," formed by citizens of the city because of dissatisfaction with Confederate military preparations to defend the city, complained to President Davis that the inability of the Navy Department to meet its debts was retarding naval construction. Mallory placed the blame squarely upon the Treasury Department.[30]

The attempt by the secretary of the treasury to substitute government bonds in place of Treasury notes to pay off debts also invoked criticism from the naval secretary:

> I am aware, of course, that in meeting the requisitions of this Department you are compelled to pay in bonds and notes, but the general character of its expenditures do not admit of the use of bonds to any great extent, and they

must be paid in notes, *or not paid at all*. A small proportion
only of bonds to notes, not more generally than one fifth,
can be paid out. This is what I have so frequently and
earnestly urged; and I have done so from the conviction
that the credit of the Department and its ability to build
and equip vessels and to conduct its operations generally,
have been crippled by the practice of the Treasury Department in sending to our Disbursing officers bonds
which they could not use to pay debts for which notes
were specially required on the face of the requisitions. . . .
Parties holding the articles, the labor and materials, we re-
quire, refuse bonds and will sell only for notes; and if the
Treasury continues to issue to them bonds which they
cannot use, in lieu of the notes which they contract to
pay—the debts of the Department remain unpaid—its
credit fails. The price of every article it attempts to purchase is at once raised and its operations are crippled.[31]

During the last year of the war Mallory was still complaining about the tardiness of the Treasury Department in
providing funds. "Much injury has accrued to the service at
the naval station at Charleston from the difficulty in receiving
Naval Warrants to fill requisitions made by me upon your
Department," he wrote in August 1864. "Parties have refused
to sell articles . . . because they could not be paid for them.
The employees upon the Iron Clad Gun Boats now building
have suffered much from the irregularity of their payments
arising from nonreceipt of money. . . ."[32]

Although Treasury notes were scarce in1862, production
rapidly reached the point where the government instead of facing
a shortage of negotiable paper, confronted an overabundance. In
fact, paper currency became so plentiful that it resulted in the
greatest inflation ever seen in America with the possible exception of the American Revolution.[33] Inevitably, as wages fell
behind prices, dissatisfied workers followed the age-old remedy
of striking. In November 1861 workers in the New Orleans
shipyards went out on strike, resulting in a halt of naval

construction until the shipbuilders would agree to a $1.00 a day increase. On June 8, 1863, Mallory wrote the Secretary of Treasury to provide the navy with additional funds immediately. "Mechanics on the *Raleigh* [ironclad under construction at Wilmington] refuse to work until paid," he wrote; "Borrowed five thousand dollars for present emergency." Lieutenant McCorkle, in charge of the ordnance at Atlanta, wrote Catesby ap R. Jones in 1864 that "my men have struck for ten dollars a day because Governor Brown, the miserable devil, has given that price to the men in State and road shops. . . ."[34] Another officer wrote to Jones that when his men laid down their tools and refused to work "unless I increased their wages, I at once ordered the arrest and confinement of all soldiers and conscripts." "But the exempts," he added, "I simply [fired]."[35] Even Buchanan at Mobile, who generaly had few labor problems, was threatened with a strike if overdue wages were not paid. The wages were paid, but shortly afterwards the workers struck anyway because of an order which added an hour to their daily stint. In another case a number of carpenters struck at Selma and travelled to Mobile looking for work. Marines met their boat, arrested them, and hauled them off to the guard house. When the admiral threatened to turn the recalcitrant workers over to the conscription officer, they agreed to return to work. Buchanan evidently was not satisfied, for in August 1863 he had all of the workers in the shipyards in Mobile, Montgomery, and Selma, conscripted and detailed to work under his orders.[36]

Work was seriously delayed also because the laborers were organized into military units for local defense. This held up completion of naval vessels at New Orleans, Richmond, and elsewhere. The manufacture of machinery and naval ordnance was affected too. Lieutenant Robert Minor, in charge of the naval ordnance works at Richmond, wrote in July 1864, that "wrought or cast iron bolts for the seven inch rifle gun can not be supplied by the naval ordnance workshops as the employees . . . are now in the field." The frequent interruptions at Richmond because workers had to man the city's defenses, "seriously retarded, and in some instances en-

tirely suspended, the progress of important works," reported
the naval secretary to Davis in the spring of 1864. In this case,
as in many others, Mallory appealed directly to the president
to order the workers released from military duty.[37] In most
of these cases Davis followed his general policy of referring
the matter back to the secretary of war.

There can be no question that the manpower problem
hurt the Confederacy in its war efforts. In trying to fill her
constantly-depleting armies, the South had to draw off from
the economic front a much higher proportion of manpower
than did the North. The Confederate government tried by
exemption and detail to fill the gaps left in labor, but the
efforts were half-hearted and unsuccessful. Toward the end
of 1864 General Josiah Gorgas, in charge of the army's ordnance bureau, complained that, whereas two years earlier
there had been no machinery, there was now a surplus but
no one to run it.

Conclusions

IN THIS STUDY the author has examined the efforts of the Confederacy to build and outfit warships. The major difficulties encountered by Southerners in developing this war industry include exploitation of essential raw materials; transportation of raw iron, plating, and other crucial items to the various naval facilities; the acquisition and retention of competent and adequate labor; the development of shipyards and related facilities; policies of the Confederate government, especially the military services and their overall effects on the shipbuilding industry as a whole on the one hand—and the course of the war on the other.

Confederate President Davis had little interest in naval affairs, and Mallory ran the department with little interference throughout the war. The Confederate navy did not have a chief of naval operations or its equivalent, and strategic decisions as well as those of policy were made by the secretary. Mallory, however, relied heavily upon a number of naval officers for advice, and performed well as a wartime secretary, considering the problems that he faced.

The Confederate government began the war with a strong *laissez-faire* attitude toward industry, including shipbuilding. The inability of private enterprise to supply the South's needs resulted in a modification of this policy. The Navy Department developed new facilities for the construction of ships, and manufacture of ordnance, ordnance stores, rope, and marine machinery. The government also influenced production by assigning or withholding labor, and by permitting or denying transportation. Nevertheless, government regulation of industry did not prevent intense competition from developing over the procurement of raw materials, acquisition and retention of labor, and the use of railroads. Government control was frequently too little or too late and in many cases discouraged industrial production.

Shipbuilding was only one of the industries that the South had to develop in order to conduct a successful war. But it inevitably affected and was affected by the entire industrial program of the Confederacy. It is incorrect to say, as many historians have, that the South lacked manufacturing facilities to provide weapons, including warships. Adequate facilities were available in 1861 or were developed as the war progressed. The Confederacy's weakness was not inadequate facilities, but the inability to exploit those that were available. There were never enough raw materials, especially iron, to meet the need of the manufacturing establishments. Tredegar and other foundries and rolling mills developed the capacity to provide armor and boiler plate, machinery, guns, and other metal parts for warships, but never were these facilities used to their full potential. Pig iron production enabled Tredegar to operate at no more than one-third of plant capacity during the four years of war. Even when pig iron was available, production was limited because of the shortage of fuel. The president of Tredegar wrote the naval secretary in March 1863: "We have iron to run six puddling furnaces instead of twenty and these have been stopped much for want of coal."[1] The South had supplies of coal and iron in Virginia, North Carolina, Georgia, and Alabama, but the Confederacy was never able to produce adequate amounts for its industries. The fact that after the spring of 1862 the naval shipbuilding program concentrated on ironclads made the problem of obtaining raw iron even more crucial. At least ten vessels-of-war were destroyed on the stocks while waiting for their armor.

The South's inadequate transportation system played a major role in delaying—often fatally—the completion of warships. In March 1862 the builders of the *Mississippi* in New Orleans reported to Mallory that construction on the vessel was being delayed because of the "nonreceipt of iron . . . from Atlanta." The iron was at Mobile but no rolling stock was available. Once flat cars became available the movement of iron was resumed, but the last shipment did not arrive at the building site until April 23, twenty-four hours before Farragut opened the battle for the city. In March 1864 the naval officer supervising construction of the ironclad *Neuse* in North Carolina wrote: "The *Neuse* floats not— the first course of iron is complete—the second fairly begun . . . the stop is at Wilmington, where there are several car loads of iron waiting transportation." When Mallory reminded the War Department of the disaster that might befall the vessel if transportation were not provided for the iron, the quartermaster general replied, "at present forage and food necessary for our armies in the field demand our entire transportation." In April the vessel's builder wrote, "you have no idea of the delay in forwarding iron to this place—it may be unavoidable, but I don't believe it. At one time twenty one days passed without my receiving a piece."[2]

Transportation of raw materials to the manufacturing establishments was just as insufficient. Catesby ap R. Jones, while commanding the naval ordnance facility at Selma, Alabama, wrote: "The principal difficulty in coal now arises, not from its scarcity . . . but from the limited means of transportation." Tredegar, the Confederacy's most important industrial establishment, was unable to obtain a single ton of Alabama iron primarily because transportation was not available. Only small amounts of Georgia, Tennessee, and North and South Carolina iron reached Richmond.

The decentralization of shipbuilding and related facilities in 1862 compounded the transportation problem. Shipyards were in various localities; ordnance works, machinery works, rolling mills, etc. in other places. In October 1862 Colin McRae, at that time an agent for the Niter and Mining Bureau in Alabama, requested the Shelby Iron Company to forward twenty-five tons of pig iron to the naval works at Columbus, Georgia. Two-thirds of this order was held up at Selma because of inadequate transportation facilities. On October 31 McRae sent an urgent message to the army quartermaster at Selma to ship the iron immediately, since "this iron . . . is required to complete the Engines and machinery for floating batteries [under construction] at this place. . . ."[3] The ore was sent by rail to Selma, transferred to riverboats and carried to Montgomery, loaded back on railroad cars and sent to Columbus. The completed machinery for two ironclads at Selma had to be returned in the same manner. A boiler for an ironclad at Wilmington was taken off an old steamer there, sent to Columbus, Georgia, to be modified, and then transported back to Wilmington for installation.

The navy inadvertently contributed to the transportation problem by seizing railroad iron for rolling into armor plate. Generally lines in use were not tampered with, but because of the practice of confiscating or purchasing unused rails, replacements were not available when needed.

An inadequate labor force seriously hampered naval building, although the problem was primarily the result of mishandling the available manpower. Lieutenant John Brooke clearly pointed this out to the naval secretary in April 1864:

> There are in the Southern States more than a sufficient number of mechanics to work these [ordnance] establishments to their full capacity and to supply all the heavy ordnance required to arm the ironclads and other vessels completed and building, and to furnish guns for the defense of our ports. . . . But these men have been swept into the Army en masse and their services can only be obtained by special and individual detail. Months are generally occupied in the process, and so rarely are applications granted that the services of not more than one in ten are secured. . . .[4]

There were ship carpenters, mechanics, and caulkers in the various sea and river ports in 1861 to provide the nucleus for a labor force, but many of these were Northerners or foreigners who left the South when fighting broke out. The remainder volunteered or were swept into the army by military conscription. An unsympathetic attitude by President Davis, the War Department, and a high percentage of army officers toward exemption and detail handicapped naval building throughout the war. Men were obtained, but too often they were untrained in shipbuilding, foundry work, and other skills. The labor shortage affected not only the number of vessels constructed but also their seaworthiness.

Writers have emphasized the "makeshift" or "home-made" qualities of the Confederate vessels. Bern Anderson in his recent study of the naval aspects of the Civil War, *By Sea and By River*, suggests that Southern officers were realistic enough to see that their "makeshift" warships were no match for the vessels of their opponents, and this created a sense of futility in attempting to accomplish an almost hopeless task. There is some basis for this: the *Arkansas'* executive officer called her "a humbug, and badly constructed"; the *Missouri's* designated commanding officer refused to take command since "the damned vessel would sink." Shortages of essential materials accounted for many of their weaknesses. The use of green timber and cotton caulking resulted in serious leakage in a number of the vessels. Pumps had to be manned twenty-four hours a day on the *Savannah* to keep her afloat. The *North Carolina* sank at her moorings because there was no copper to sheath her bottom against worms. Most of the Confederate warships surrendered to the Union navy at the end of the war were condemned and sold as scrap because of badly worm-eaten bottoms.

The marine machinery used on the vessels built within the Confederacy was notoriously inadequate and constantly in need of repair. Although river boats and steamships provided many warships with their engines, boilers, shafts, etc., an undetermined number were equipped with power and propulsion plants manufactured in Southern machine works.

Confederate naval officers voiced more criticism of and had less faith in their vessels' machinery than anything else, and with justification. All were slow and many could not even stem a strong current. Engines frequently broke down at crucial times—the *Arkansas* was lost because of this.

The navy was more fortunate in arming its vessels than in providing adequate motive power for them. Under the capable leadership of men such as John Brooke and Catesby ap R. Jones, the production of naval ordnance increased steadily throughout the war. There was really never a shortage of guns, although some ships never had full batteries and others were armed with mixed batteries.

From 1861 to 1865 the Southern Confederacy converted, contracted for, or laid down within its borders at least 150 warships. Of this number approximately one-third were steamers converted into gunboats (including the state navies), one-third were wooden gunboats, and one-third were ironclads. At least five wooden and twenty-two armored vessels, built from the keel up, were completed. The remainder were not completed partly because of the scarcity of essential materials and workmen, partly because of the dispersion of shipbuilding facilities, and partly because of the withdrawal of military forces from building areas, necessitating destruction of ships and yards.

Military, geographic, and political reasons were primarily responsible for the dispersal of naval facilities throughout the Confederacy. The major ship construction centers in the South—Norfolk, New Orleans, and Pensacola—were captured by Union forces in 1862. The Navy Department had to utilize small yards or develop new ones. These yards were located on rivers, far enough upstream to protect them from Northern military operations, and close to timber resources. All of the Confederate states were threatened by amphibious attacks, real or imaginary, and it was therefore necessary to develop naval defenses in every state. As the war progressed and the Confederacy was gradually occupied, naval establishments and ships under construction were destroyed to prevent their capture and use by the North. If time had allowed, the Confederacy would have completed many more warships, but it is doubtful that this would have altered the final outcome of the war.

Notes

Introduction

1 Charles P. Rowland, *The Confederacy* (Chicago, 1960) pp. 35-36.

The Program

1 The standard biography of Mallory is Joseph T. Durkin, *Stephen Mallory: Confederate Navy Chief* (Chapel Hill, 1954).

2 Frank E. Vandiver, *Rebel Brass: The Confederate Command System* (Baton Rouge, 1956), p. 133.

3 *Durkin*, p. 133.

4 John B. Jones, *A Rebel War Clerk's Diary at the Confederate States Capital*, 2 vols. (Philadelphia, 1886), I, 21.

5 Quoted in Virgil C. Jones, *The Civil War At Sea* (New York, 1960), I, 41.

6 J. Thomas Scharf, *History of the Confederate States Navy* (New York, 1887), pp. 24-25.

7 These vessels were the *Savannah* (two guns), *Huntress* (one gun), *Lady Davis* (two guns), *Firefly* (one gun), *Winslow* (two guns), *Raleigh* (one gun), *Beaufort* (one gun), *Patrick Henry* [ex-*Yorktown*] (ten guns), and *Jamestown* (two guns).

8 April 26, 1861, *Official Records of the Union and Confederate Navies in the War of the Rebellion, 31 vols.* (Washington, D. C., 1894-1927), Ser. II, Vol. II, 54. Hereafter cited as *Official Records, Navies.*

9 *Ibid.*, pp. 67-69.

10 Report of the Secretary of the Navy, July 18, 1861, *ibid.*, p. 79.

11 *Ibid.*, Vol. I, 791, 792.

12 Investigation of the Navy Department, *ibid.*, pp. 781-782.

13 February 27, 1862, *ibid.*, Vol. II, 152.

14 *Ibid.*, pp. 117-118. For a detailed account of Maury's gunboats see Frances L. Williams' impressive biography, *Matthew Fontaine Maury: Scientist of the Sea* (New Brunswick, 1963), pp. 382-390.

15 To Gilbert Elliott, William F. Martin Papers, Southern Historical Collection, University of North Carolina Library, Chapel Hill.

16 There were probably others, but these are the only ones that can be identified. Mallory to Governor John Milton, October 15, 26, November 2, 19, and 28, 1861, John Milton Letterbooks, Florida Historical Society Collection, University of South Florida, Tampa; Mallory to Ebenezer Farrand, October 10, 1861, in Confederate Subject and Area File, Record Group 45, The National Archives, hereafter cited as SA File; Augustus McLaughlin to Bolling Baker, March 1, 1862, SA File; Farrand to Mallory, April 11, 1862, *Official Records, Navies*, Ser. I, Vol. XXII, 845-846; Mallory to C. G. Memminger, August 24, 1861, Confederate Treasury Department Records, Record Group 365, The National Archives; Mallory to Farrand, November 20, 1861, and Josiah Tattnall to Farrand, January 31, 1862, Ebenezer Farrand folder, ZB File, Division of Naval History, Navy Department; Mallory to James H. Warner, December 17, 1861, James H. Warner folder, ZB File.

17 Charles Graves to Cousin, March 2, 1862, Charles I. Graves Papers, Southern Historical Collection, University of North Carolina Library.

18 *Official Records, Navies*, Ser. II, Vol. II, 152; *ibid.*, Vol. I, 796.

19 William N. Still, Jr., "Confederate Naval Policy and the Ironclad," *Civil War History*, IX (1963), 153.

20 Because of incomplete records it is nearly impossible to estimate the number laid down in naval yards or under the supervision of naval officers. Evidently there were also verbal and unofficial agreements made by Mallory with various individuals for the construction of gunboats. See memorandum of Mallory dated March 17, 1862, SA File. For the contracts see the appendix to *Report of Evidence Taken Before a Joint Special Committee of Both Houses of the Confederate Congress, To Investigate the Affairs of the Navy Department* (Richmond, 1863.)

21 *Official Records, Navies*, Ser. I, Vol. XXII, 794.

22 See *Dictionary of American Fighting Ships* (Washington, D. C., 1963), II, 587, for a list of these vessels.

23 January 19, 1862, *Official Records, Navies*, Ser. I, Vol. XVII, 160-161.

24 Correspondence concerning the building of the "torpedo ram" can be found in the Letterbooks of the Department of South

Carolina and Georgia, Record Group 109, The National Archives. Included is a long detailed report written by Lee to Beauregard on February 8, 1864. See also Beauregard to Francis W. Pickens, October 8, 1862, *The War of the Rebellion: A Compilation of the Official Records of the Union and Confederate Armies*, 130 vols. (Washington, D. C., 1880-1901), Ser. I, Vol. XIV, 631, hereafter cited as *Official Records;* and Milton F. Perry, *Infernal Machines: The Story of Confederate Submarine and Mine Warfare* (Baton Rouge, 1965), pp. 63-80.

25 Perry, pp. 87-89.

26 *Baltic* Construction Papers, Military Records Division, Naval Records, File 34 Department of Archives and History, Montgomery, Alabama.

27 James Carter contacted William Bee & Company of Charleston about building three blockade runners, but there is no evidence that they were actually constructed. See February 10, 1864, William Bee & Company Papers, South Carolina Historical Society, Charleston.

28 The best of many accounts of the Confederate submarines is Perry, *Infernal Machines*, pp. 90-108.

Facilities

1 A substantial part of this chapter with extensive documentation has appeared in William N. Still, Jr., "Facilities for the Construction of War Vessels in the Confederacy," *Journal of Southern History,* XXXI (1965), 285-304.

2 Charles B. Dew, *Ironmaker to the Confederacy: Joseph R. Anderson and the Tredegar Iron Works* (New Haven, 1966), p. 12.

3 The Offices of Order and Detail, Ordnance and Hydrography, Provisions and Clothing, and Medicine and Surgery. For the administration of the Confederate Navy Department see Tom H. Wells, "The Confederate Navy: A Study in Organization" (diss., Emory University, 1963).

4 Wells, 113.

5 Investigation of the Navy Department, *Official Records, Navies,* Ser. II, Vol. I, 803; Thomas J. Wertenbaker, *Norfolk: Historic Southern Port* (Durham, 1931), pp. 164-165, 207-209; John W. H. Porter, *A Record of Events in Norfolk County, Virginia* (Portsmouth, Va., 1892), pp. 334-335.

6 John H. Neill, Jr., "Shipbuilding in Confederate New Orleans" (master's thesis, Tulane University, 1940), p. 47; *Report of Evidence* p. 75; William M. Parks, "Building a Warship in the Southern Confederacy," *United States Naval Institute Proceedings,* LXIX (1923), 1299-1307; Harrison Trexler, "The Confederate Navy and the Fall of New Orleans," *Southwest Review* (1933), 88-102; James M.

Merrill, "Confederate Shipbuilding in New Orleans," *Journal of Southern History*, XXVII (1962), 87-93; Charles G. Summersell, *The Cruise of the C.S.S. Sumter* (Tuscaloosa, 1965), pp. 21-22.

7 Walter Chandler, "The Memphis Navy Yard," *West Tennessee Historical Society Papers*, I (1947), 70-71; Gerald M. Capers, Jr., *The Biography of a River Town* (Chapel Hill, 1939), pp. 82-84.

8 To General John H. Forney, May 14, 1862, *Official Records*, Ser. I, Vol. VI, 660.

9 Anderson to Forrest, November 5, 1861, letterbook, Tredegar Rolling Mill and Foundry Collection, 1861-1865, Virginia State Library, Richmond. See also Anderson to Forrest, Nov. 7, 9, 19, 22, 23, 1861, letterbook, Tredegar Rolling Mill and Foundry Collection, 1861-1865; and Dew, p. 118.

10 Voucher to pay Anderson, Nov. 2, 1861, SA File; Anderson to Forrest, Nov. 7, 1861, letterbook, Tredegar Rolling Mill and Foundry Collection, 1861-1865; George M. Brooke, Jr., "John Mercer Brooke," (2 vols., diss., University of North Carolina, 1955), II, 796.

11 Court of Inquiry, *Official Records*, Ser. I, Vol. VI, 626-627.

12 Quoted in a letter from Mallory to the Secretary of War, March 11, 1864, *ibid.*, Vol. XXXIII, 1218-1219. A month before two carloads of plates for the ironclad *Neuse* on the way from Atlanta to Wilmington disappeared and the flag officer had several naval officers riding the rails trying to find out what happened to them. Robert Minor to wife, February 11, 1864, Minor Family Papers, Va. Historical Society.

13 They were destroyed in May 1863 when a Federal expedition pushed up the river as far as Yazoo City. Porter to Welles, May 24, 1863, David D. Porter Papers, Library of Congress. See also Mallory to Weldon and McFarland, September 16, 1862, SA File; Sheppard to Nixon, October 11, 1862, SA File.

14 There is very little information on most of these yards. Scattered information, however, can be found under the various categories (yards, ship construction, etc.) in the SA File. See also the Francis W. Dawson Papers, Duke University Library, for the quotation on "Rocketts", and the Admiral Franklin Buchanan letterbook, 1862-1863, Southern Historical Collection, University of North Carolina Library, for information on the yard at Oven Bluff, Alabama; and the Edward J. Means letterbook, Department of Archives, Louisiana State University Library, Baton Rouge, for information on the yard near Marion Court House, South Carolina.

15 Merrill, "Confederate Shipbuilding in New Orleans," p. 89.

16 For the importance of this industrial establishment to the Confederacy see Dew's *Ironmaker to the Confederacy*.

17 *Ibid.*, p. 117.

18 McRae to Jones, November 5, 1862, in Shelby Iron Company Papers, University of Alabama Library, University; Edwin Layton,

"Colin J. McRae and the Selma Arsenal," *Alabama Review*, XVIII (1966), 132-133.

19 McRae to Gorgas, in Colin J. McRae Papers, Alabama Department of Archives and History, Montgomery.

20 Wells, p. 51.

21 Brooke, "John Mercer Brooke," II, 849.

22 *Ibid.*, p. 799.

23 Dew, p. 86; Kathleen Bruce, *Virginia Iron Manufacture in the Slave Era* (New York, 1931), p. 262.

24 SA File.

25 Other facilities established included grain mills, a bakery, and a box factory, established by Nelson and Asa Tift at Albany, Georgia, and a whiskey distillery "to be used by the Medical Purveyor and as rations," at Augusta, Georgia. Charleston *Daily Courier*, February 22, 1864; Howell to Hunter, November 18, 1863, William W. Hunter Papers, Howard-Tifton Memorial Library, Tulane University, New Orleans, Louisiana.

26 Charles Girard, *A Visit to the Confederate States of America*, ed. W. Stanley Hoole (Tuscaloosa, 1963), p. 55.

Materials

1 Dew, *Ironmaker to the Confederacy*, p. 178.

2 John J. Peck to Butler, February 23, 1864, *Official Records*, Ser. I, Vol. XXXIII, 589.

3 U.S. Census Office, Eighth Census, 1860, *Manufactures of the United States in 1860* (Washington, D.C., 1865), pp. clxxvii, clxx, and clxxxiii. One authority states that Alabama had seven or possibly eight. Joseph H. Woodward, II, *Alabama Blast Furnaces* (Woodward, Alabama, 1940), p. 18.

4 Clark, I, 499; John G. Van Deusen, *Economic Bases of Disunion in South Carolina* (New York, 1928), p. 286; see also the works by Armes and Bruce. Virginia produced only 11,646 tons in 1860, and most of this came from that part of the state that would become West Virginia.

5 Dew, p. 175.

6 *Ibid.*

7 Anderson to Mallory, March 25, May 31, 1863; Anderson & Company to George Minor, December 6, 1862, letterbook, Tredegar Rolling Mill and Foundry Papers, 1861-1865. See also Jones, *A Rebel War Clerk's Diary*, II, 195; and Dew, p. 265.

8 *Official Records, Navies*, Ser. II, Vol. II, 73-74. The time element varied—one company had five years to deliver its quota, but the usual time was three years. The Shelby Iron Company contract provided for no definite quota, but it agreed to supply iron and

iron products worth $1,000,000 in 1862, $1,000,000 in 1863, and the same in 1864.

9 Niter and Mining Bureau records, Record Group 109; General Order Number 85, Adjutant and Inspector General's Office, June 16, 1863, *Official Records*, Ser. IV, Vol. II, 594-595.

10 For the importation of iron and other minerals see William Diamond, "Imports of the Confederate Government from Europe and Mexico," *Journal of Southern History*, VI (1940), 483.

11 To Roberts, June 17, 1862, War Department Papers, Record Group 109.

12 Arthur C. Cole, *The Irrepressible Conflict, 1850-1865* (New York, 1934), p. 300; Richmond *Dispatch*, September 30, 1863. Mallory requested that the rails in the Customs House yard at Charleston and the mint at New Orleans be turned over to the navy. Mallory to Memminger, May 5, 1863, and April 11, 1862, Confederate Treasury Department Papers, Record Group 365. As in most Southern states Georgia was a stockholder in railroad companies in the state. Georgia owned five-elevenths of the stock of the Atlantic & Gulf Railroad. When the navy persisted in confiscating rails from this line, Governor Brown protested and continued doing so without success. See Brown to Colonel Headley, March, 16, 1863; John Scrivner to Brown, March 14, 1863; Mallory to Seddon, April 22, 1863—all in War Department Papers, Record Group 109.

13 McCorkle to Jones, July 31, 1863, SA File. See also Miner to Mallory, November 24, 1863, *Official Records, Navies*, Ser. I, Vol. XIII, 816-817; Davis to Messrs. Hiram Roberts and others, July 31, 1862, Rowland, V, 305; George Mercer Diary, Southern Historical Collection; Mercer to Randolph, August 5, 1862, and Mallory to Randolph, July 25, 1862, in War Department Papers, Record Group 109. The petition is located in the Jefferson Davis Papers, Miami University Library, Oxford, Ohio. A letter from Mallory to Davis concerning the controversy is also in this collection, dated July 31, 1862.

14 Gift to Milton, May 4, 1863; Milton to Seddon, May 10, 1863; Finegan to Milton, May 12, 1863; Milton to Finegan, May 21, 1863; Milton to Yulee, May 30, 1863; and Yulee to Milton, May 23, 1863—all in the John Milton Letterbooks. See also Gift to E. Shackelford, May 14, 1863, Ellen Shackleford Gift Papers, Southern Historical Collection; Harriet Castlen, *Hope Bids Me Onward* (Savannah, 1945), p. 118; Black, pp. 208-213; John E. Johns, *Florida During the Civil War* (Gainesville, 1963), pp. 138-139.

15 Bonham to Beauregard, February 6, 1863, Francis W. Pickens Papers, Duke University Library, Durham; Jones, p. 301; Lee to Harris, February 3, 1863, *Official Records*, Ser. I, Vol. XIV, 761.

16 Copy of letter that Lieutenant James W. Cooke (in charge of building the *Albemarle*) wrote Mallory in the Vance letterbook, North Carolina Department of Archives and History. Cooke

later sent one of the contractors of the vessel, Gilbert Elliott, to try to get the iron. Elliott blamed Flag Officer William Lynch for all the trouble, calling him "incompetent, inefficient and almost imbecile." Elliott to Vance, January 24, 1864, Zebulon B. Vance Papers and Letterbooks, North Carolina Department of Archives and History, Raleigh. See also John G. Barrett, *The Civil War in North Carolina* (Chapel Hill, 1963), pp. 214-215. Evidently he is referring to the North Carolina Railroad that linked Charlotte to Goldsboro by way of Raleigh. There was no Charlotte & North Carolina line.

17 Lynch to Vance, May 13, 1863; Vance to Lynch, May 18, 1863; Davis A. Barnes, aide-de-camp to the governor, to W. W. Guion, May 18, 1863—all in the Vance letterbook, North Carolina Department of Archives and History.

18 *Official Records,* Ser. IV, Vol. II, 365.

19 Jones, II, 132.

20 *Official Records,* Ser. IV, Vol. I, 988-989.

21 Mallory to Brown, April 11, 1862, Mallory to Davis, September 24, 1862, *Official Records, Navies,* Ser. II, Vol. II, 183, 274.

22 Dew, p. 144. In February and in August 1861 Congress authorized the president or the secretary of war to make advance payments up to one-third the value of contracts for cannon.

23 St. John to Seddon, October 1, 1864, *Official Records,* Ser. IV, Vol. III, 695. A search of available records has not determined the total number of blast furnaces in any Confederate state during the war years, nor the amount of iron ore produced. Tredegar, however, produced only 3,127 long tons of iron from its furnaces in 1864. Dew, p. 166.

24 If the Confederacy had survived as a nation it is problematical as to whether or not the iron industry could have been developed. A relatively important iron industry with outside capital was developed in the Birmingham area in the late nineteenth century, however.

25 January 4, 1865, Letterbook of the Office of Ordnance and Hydrography, Record Group 109.

26 Copper was taken from sunken and wrecked ships—Confederate, Union, and blockade runners—whenever possible. See Myers to Jones, August 14, 1864, SA File. See also Diamond, "Imports of the Confederate Government from Europe and Mexico," 483; Peet to Mallory, August 29, 1861, *Official Records, Navies,* Ser. II, Vol. II, 93; Brooke, "John Mercer Brooke," II, 891-892.

27 Tucker to Beauregard, January 10, 1864, Department of South Carolina and Georgia letterbooks, Record Group 109; McCorkle to Tattnall, August 23, 1863, Savannah Squadron, CSN, Correspondence, Emory University Library, Atlanta. See also Tucker to Beauregard, August 2, 1863, *Official Records,* Ser. I, Vol. XXVIII, Pt. 1, 382; Beauregard to Tucker, January 13, 1864, *Ibid.,* Vol.

XXXV, Pt. 1, 523. Wood was frequently used as fuel by Confederate ships.

28   For the Wilmington controversy see *Official Records,* Ser. I, Vol. XLVI, Pt. II, 1156-1158. For the Trans-Mississippi trouble see Carter to Surget, February 15, 1863, Carter Letterbook, Record Group 45.

29   Jones to Lee, September 17, 1864, SA File. See also W. H. Blake, "Coal Barging in Wartime 1861-1865," *Gulf State Historical Magazine,* I (1901), 409-410.

30   Howard N. Eavenson, *The First Century and a Quarter of American Coal Industry* (Pittsburgh, 1942), p. 299; John De Bree to Mallory, August 14, 1862, *Official Records,* Ser. II, Vol. II, 249-250.

31   Forrest to Mitchell, September 10, 1862, John K. Mitchell Papers, Virginia Historical Society, Richmond.

32   Jones to Warner, October 15, 1864 SA File. McCorkle to Tattnall, August 23, 1863, Savannah Squadron, CSN Correspondence.

33   Report of the Office of Orders and Detail, October 31, 1864, *Official Records, Navies* Ser. II, Vol. 753-754.

34   Other timbers used by the Confederates in shipbuilding include the cypress, poplar, black walnut, and ash. For shipbuilding in the South see John G. S. Hutchins, *The American Maritime Industries and Public Policy, 1789-1914* (Cambridge, Mass., 1941), pp. 75-93; and *1880 Census, Hall Report on the Shipbuilding Industry of the United States,* pp. 246-248.

35   *Official Records, Navies,* Ser. II, Vol. II, 54.

Labor

1   An exception was the effort of the builder of the two ironclads at Memphis to locate qualified ship carpenters. He advertised in newspapers in Mobile, Charleston, Nashville, New Orleans, St. Louis, and elsewhere with very little success. Investigation of the Navy Department, *Official Records, Navies* Ser. II, Vol. I, 783.

2   There also seems to have been an exodus of mechanics with the outbreak of hostilities. An undetermined number of skilled laborers in the South prior to 1861 were Northerners, and many of them returned to the North. Mary E. Massey, *Ersatz in the Confederacy* (Columbia, 1952), p. 27; Capers, p. 143; Dew, pp. 90-91.

3   Walker to Mallory, Aug. 30, 1861, War Department Papers, Record Group 109.

4   A. T. Bledsoe to Mallory, December 19 and 28, 1861, War Department Papers, Record Group 109. Not all army officers refused to cooperate. General Benjamin Huger asked and was granted permission to discharge "such persons as you think will be more useful as mechanics in the Navy Yard than as soldiers in the field." Ran-

dolph to Huger, April 2, 1862, War Department Papers, Record Group 109.

5 January 15, 1862, War Department Papers, Record Group 109.

6 Stephen R. Mallory Diary, Southern Historical Collection.

7 Yearns, pp. 84-85; Ramsdell, "The Control of Manufacturing by the Confederate Government," 231-236.

8 To Silas Cooper, October 21, 1863, *Official Records*, Ser. I, Vol. XXIX, Pt. 2, 798.

9 Seddon to Mallory, February 24, 1863, War Department Papers, Record Group 109. See also Whiting to Pinckney, November 27, 1864, and Whiting to Porter, October 13, 1864, in W. H. C. Whiting Letterbook, Record Group 109.

10 McRae Collection.

11 Weldon to Pemberton, February 14, 1863, Thomas Weldon folder, Citizens File, Record Group 109; Weldon to Breckinridge, August 3, 1862, Weldon folder; Gardner to Pemberton, February 6, 1863, General John C. Pemberton Papers, Record Group 109; Ware to Nixon, August 26 and December 2, 1862, Thomas Ware Letterbooks, Record Group 45.

12 McCorkle to Brooke, May 7, 1864, *Official Records*, Ser. IV, Vol. III, 522. See also Seddon to Mallory, March 15, 1864, War Department Papers, Record Group 109. For Ramsay's report see May 5, 1864, *Official Records*, Ser. IV, Vol. III, 521-522. For the report of the Selma works see Jones to Brooke, May 14, 1864, *Ibid.*, p. 523.

13 Carter to Holmes, April 20, 1863, Carter Letterbook, Record Group 45; Buchanan to Pemberton, December 9, 1862, Buchanan Letterbook; Shirley & DeHaven to Hart, November 9, 1863, John Shirley folder, Citizens File, Record Group 109.

14 April 20, 1864, *Official Records, Navies*, Ser. II, Vol. 637. In October, 1863, Mallory had written to the secretary of war that "officers of the Navy complain that the employees under their supervision and in the service of the Navy, are being arrested and held by officers of the conscript service who disregard the certificates held by such employees . . ." (to Seddon, October 5, 1863, War Department Papers, Record Group 109). See also Parker to Mallory, Oct. 3, 1863, War Department Papers, Record Group 109.

15 April 20, 1864, *Official Records, Navies*, Ser. II, Vol. II, 637.

16 Like most Confederate figures, those concerning labor are sketchy and misleading. There is no way of determining the number of foreign and Northern born mechanics in the Confederacy, although Ella Lonn estimates that most of the mechanics and munition workers were foreign born. Ella Lonn, *Foreigners in the Confederate Army and Navy* (Chapel Hill, 1940), p. 338. See also Dew, p. 234.

17 Raphael Semmes, *Memoirs of Service Afloat during the War between the States* (New York, 1869), p. 83.

18 Bulloch, II, 231-233; Brooke to Jones, September 16, 1864, SA File:
    Albert B. Moore, *Conscription and Conflict in the Confederacy*
    (New York, 1924), p. 61; Mallory to Bulloch, October 8, 1862,
    Official Records, Navies, Ser. II, Vol. II, 280. Jefferson Davis to
    J. E. Brown, September 19, 1864, *Confederate Records of the State
    of Georgia,* 6 vols. (Atlanta, 1909-1911), III, 623; Lonn, pp. 339-340.

19 Clark, II, 51; Dew, pp. 234-235.

20 Weldon to Pettus, October 14, 15, 1862, January 26 and February 25,
    1863, Mississippi's Governors' Papers, Department of Archives and
    History, Jackson; James Hamilton to McFarland, January 15, 1863,
    Mississippi Adjutant Letterbook, 1863, Department of Archives
    and History, Jackson; Pettus to Pemberton, n.d., Pemberton Papers,
    Record Group 109.

21 Mallory to Acting Constructor William Graves, March 30, 1863,
    SA File. There are a number of travel vouchers in the SA file for
    carpenters, constructors, etc., as they applied for reimbursement
    for travelling from facility to facility. See also Mallory to Acting
    Constructor William Hope, September 13, 1862, and Lynch to
    Master Builder J. H. Yatt, October 7, 1862, in SA File.

22 Leonard P. Stavisky, "Industrialism in Ante Bellum Charleston,"
    Journal of Negro History, XXXVI (1951), 311; Charles H.
    Wesley, *Negro Labor in the United States, 1850-1925* (New York,
    1927), pp. 34-36. Sydney S. Bradford, "The Negro Ironworker in
    Ante Bellum Virginia," *Journal of Southern History,* XXV (1959),
    194-206.

23 Feb. 1, 1865, Office of Ordnance and Hydrography Letterbook,
    Record Group 109. The chief of the Niter and Mining Bureau
    reported in September 1864 that government controlled blast fur-
    naces and mining operations employed 4,301 Negroes. The naval
    ordnance works at Selma employed 310 slave and 91 free workers
    in early 1865. *Official Records,* Ser. IV, Vol. III, 696; Bell Wiley,
    Southern Negroes, 1861-1865 (New Haven, 1938), pp. 112-113.

24 September 30, 1862, McRae Collection.

25 Anderson to Mallory, December 11, 1862, letterbook, Tredegar
    Rolling Mill and Foundry Collection, 1861-1865. For rivalry between
    naval facilities in the same locality see Jones to Farrand, June 10,
    1863, Jones letterbook, Record Group 45.

26 Seddon to Mallory, October 21, 1863, War Department Papers,
    Record Group 109. The most serious examples of this rivalry oc-
    curred at Wilmington, North Carolina, between Flag Officer Lynch
    and General W. H. C. Whiting, and at Selma between Catesby
    ap R. Jones and Colonel J. L. White. For Wilmington see Whiting
    to Lynch, May 24, 25, 1863, District of Cape Fear and North
    Carolina Letterbook, Record Group 109. For Selma see the letter-
    books and papers on the naval facilities at Selma in the SA File.
    See also McCorkle to Major Wright, May 14, 1863, SA File, for
    rivalry at Atlanta.

27 "Proceedings of the Confederate Congress," *Southern Historical
    Society Papers,* Vols. XLIV-LII (1923-1959), XII, 330.

28 Richard C. Todd, *Confederate Finances* (Athens, 1954), p. 98.

29 Mallory to C. G. Memminger, February 22, 1862, Confederate Treasury Department Records, Record Group 365.

30 March 8, 1862, *Official Records, Navies*, Ser. II, Vol. II, 714-715; Committee to Davis, February 26, 1862, *Official Records*, Ser. I, Vol. VI, 831-832; Court of Inquiry, *ibid*, 575-576; Mallory to Memminger, March 1, 1862, Confederate Treasury Department Records, Record Group 365. See also Mallory to Memminger, January 11, 15, February 17, and March 24, 1862, Confederate Treasury Department Records, Record Group 365; *Official Records, Navies*, Ser. I, Vol. II, 733-738; *ibid.*, Ser. II, Vol. II, 477.

31 Mallory to Memminger, April 7, 1862, March 28, 1862, Confederate Treasury Department Papers, Record Group 365.

32 Mallory to Trenholm, August 2, 1864, Confederate Treasury Department Papers, Record Group 365; see also Mallory to Memminger, May 28, 1864, Confederate Treasury Department Papers, Record Group 365.

33 Clement Eaton, *A History of the Southern Confederacy* (New York, 1954), p. 239. For the effect that inflation had on the pay scale for mechanics and carpenters employed by the navy see Mallory to A. G. Brown, February 18, 1865, SA File.

34 N.d., *Official Records, Navies*, Ser. I, Vol. XXI, 870.

35 McGuyler to Jones, December 15, 1863, Jones Papers, Record Group 45.

36 Buchanan to Mallory, September 20, 1863, Buchanan Letterbook; Buchanan to Mitchell, June 13, 1863, Mitchell Papers; Ware to O'Neal, April 15, 1864, Ware Letterbook, Record Group 45.

37 Davis to Beauregard, December 28, 1864, Rowland, VI, 429.

Conclusions

1 Quoted in Dew, *Ironmaker to the Confederacy*, p. 267.

2 Benjamin P. Loyall to Robert Minor, Minor Family Papers.

3 McRae to Jones, October 23, 1862, Shelby Iron Company Papers; McRae to Captain Harris, October 31, 1862, McRae letterbook.

4 April 30, 1864, *Official Records, Navies*, Ser. II, Vol. II, 642.

Bibliography

Primary Materials

Manuscripts

Record Groups 45, 109, and 365 were the major manuscript sources for this study. Record Group 45 (Naval Records Collection of the Office of Naval Records and Library) includes a category known as "the Confederate Subject and Area File." A vast amount of material (letters, receipts, bills of sale, vouchers, etc.) on naval construction are found listed under various subjects such as: (A) Naval Ships: Design, Construction, etc., (B) Ordnance, (E) Engineering, (P) Bases. The Area File, collectively described as "Loose Papers Assembled from both Official and Private Sources," includes a number of important papers concerning shipbuilding. Apart from the Subject and Area File, Confederate material in Record Group 45 includes watch quarter and station bills, pay rolls, and collections of several Confederate naval officers.

Record Group 109 (War Department Collection of Confederate Records) is located in the Old Army Section. Scattered throughout this mass of documentary material (over 5,000 cubic feet of records) are hundreds of letters concerning naval matters. Unfortunately with few exceptions (the vessel file is one), the naval documents are not separately identified, and are difficult to find. This record group also includes a few papers of the Office of Ordnance and Hydrography, and the Niter and Mining Bureau. For a complete breakdown of the various categories of documents in this record groups see Elizabeth Bethel, *Preliminary Inventory of the War Department Collection of Confederate Records* (Record Group 109) (Washington, 1957).

Record Group 365 (Confederate Treasury Department Records) is located in the Legal and Fiscal Branch. Included are copies of contracts for the construction of vessels, as well as a large number of letters from Confederate Secretary of the Navy Mallory to the secretary of the treasury.

When the records which make up Record Group 45 were transferred from the Department of the Navy to the National Archives, one group of records remained in the custody of the Navy Department. Included are records concerning naval personnel, Confederate as well as United States. The files of several Confederate naval officers, such as Naval Constructor John Porter, Chief Engineer James H. Warner, Isaac N. Brown, and Jonathan Carter, contain information on naval construction. These records are classified under the heading "ZB File," and are located in the National Archives Building.

A superb guide to the official archives of the Confederate States of America is Henry P. Beers, *Guide to the Archives of the Government of the Confederate States of America* (Washington, D. C.: Government Printing Office, 1968).

Other manuscript collections consulted include:

Richard H. Bacot Papers, Department of Archives and History, Raleigh, North Carolina.

Baltic Construction Papers, Military Records Division, Naval Records, File 34, Department of Archives and History, Montgomery, Alabama.

Franklin Buchanan Letterbook, Southern Historical Collection, University of North Carolina Library, Chapel Hill.

Confederate Veteran Magazine File, Duke University Library, Durham, North Carolina.

Jefferson Davis Papers, Duke University Library, Durham, North Carolina.

Jefferson Davis Papers, Miami University Library, Oxford, Ohio.

Francis W. Dawson Papers, Duke University Library, Durham, North Carolina.

French Forrest Papers, Southern Historical Collection, University of North Carolina Library, Chapel Hill.

French Forrest Letterbooks, Virginia State Library, Richmond.

Georgia Governor's Letterbooks, 1861-1865, Department of Archives and History, Atlanta, Georgia.

Ellen Shackelford Gift Papers, Southern Historical Collection, University of North Carolina Library, Chapel Hill, North Carolina.

William A. Hoke Papers, Southern Historical Collection, University of North Carolina Library, Chapel Hill, North Carolina.

William W. Hunter Papers, Howard-Tilton Memorial Library, Tulane University, New Orleans, Louisiana.

Colin J. McRae Collection, Department of Archives and History, Montgomery, Alabama.

Stephen R. Mallory Diary, Southern Historical Collection, University of North Carolina Library, Chapel Hill, North Carolina.

William F. Martin Papers, Southern Historical Collection, University of North Carolina Library, Chapel Hill, North Carolina.

Matthew F. Maury Papers, Manuscripts Division, Library of Congress.

Edward J. Means Letterbook, Department of Archives, Louisiana State University Library, Baton Rouge, Louisiana.

George A. Mercer Diaries, Southern Historical Collection, University of North Carolina Library, Chapel Hill, North Carolina.

William P. Miles Papers, Southern Historical Collection, University of North Carolina Library, Chapel Hill, North Carolina.

John Milton Letterbooks, Florida Historical Society Collection, University of South Florida, Tampa, Florida.

George W. and Robert Minor Papers, Virginia Historical Society, Richmond, Virginia.

Minor Family Papers, Virginia Historical Society, Richmond, Virginia.

Minutes of the City Council of Columbus, Georgia, 1861-1865, Office of the Probate Judge, City Hall, Columbus, Georgia.

Mississippi's Governor's Papers, 1861-1865, Department of Archives and History, Jackson, Mississippi.

Mississippi Adjutant Letterbook, 1863, Department of Archives and History, Jackson, Mississippi.

John K. Mitchell Papers, Virginia Historical Society, Richmond, Virginia.

North Carolina Adjutant Department Letterbooks, 1861-1865, Department of Archives and History, Raleigh, North Carolina.

Francis W. Pickens Papers, Duke University Library, Durham, North Carolina.

David D. Porter Papers, Naval Historical Foundation, Manuscripts Division, Library of Congress, Washington, D. C.

John Roy Diary, Howard-Tilton Memorial Library, Tulane University, New Orleans, Louisiana.

Savannah Squadron, CSN, Correspondence, Emory University Library, Atlanta, Georgia.

Shelby Iron Company Collection, University of Alabama Library, University, Alabama.

John G. Shorter Papers, Governor's Correspondence, Department of Archives and History, Montgomery, Alabama.

Talbott and Sons Papers, Virginia Historical Society, Richmond, Virginia.

Tredegar Rolling Mill and Foundry Collection, 1861-1865, Virginia State Library, Richmond, Virginia.

Governor Zebulon B. Vance Letterbooks and Correspondence, Department of Archives and History, Raleigh, North Carolina.

William Bee & Co. Papers, South Carolina Historical Society, Charleston, S. C.

Willink Brothers Papers, Emory University Library, Atlanta, Georgia.

Books

Acts and Resolutions of the Provisional Congress of the Confederate States. Montgomery, Alabama: Shorter & Reid, 1861.

Acts of the Second Called Session, 1861, and of the First Regular Annual Session General Assembly of Alabama Held in the City of Montgomery. Montgomery: Montgomery Advertiser Book and Job Office, 1862.

Bulloch, James D. *The Secret Service of the Confederate States in Europe.* 2 vols. London: Richard Bentley & Sons, 1883.

Confederate Records of the State of Georgia. 6 vols. Atlanta: C. P. Byrd, Printer, 1909-1911.

Girard, Charles. *A Visit to the Confederate States of America,* ed. W. Stanley Hoole. Tuscaloosa: Confederate Publishing Company, 1963.

Jones, John B. *A Rebel War Clerk's Diary at the Confederate States Capital.* 2 vols. Philadelphia: J. B. Lippincott & Company, 1866.

Journal of the Congress of the Confederate States of America, 1861-1865. 7 vols. Washington, D. C.: Government Printing Office, 1904.

Journal of the Convention of the People of South Carolina, held in 1860, 1861 and 1862 together with the Ordinances, Reports, Resolutions, etc. Columbia, S. C.: R. W. Gibbes, Printer, 1863.

Kean, Robert G. *Inside the Confederate Government,* ed. Edward Younger. New York: Oxford University Press, 1957.

Official Records of the Union and Confederate Navies in the War of the Rebellion. 31 vols. Washington, D. C.: Government Printing Office, 1894-1927.

Ramsdell, Charles W. *Laws and Joint Resolutions of the Confederate Congress.* Durham: Duke University Press, 1941.

Report of Evidence Taken Before a Joint Special Committee of Both Houses of the Confederate Congress, To Investigate the Affairs of the Navy Department. Richmond: G. P. Evans & Company, 1863.

Rowland, Dunbar, *Jefferson Davis, Constitutionalist: His Letters, Papers and Speeches.* 10 vols. Jackson, Mississippi: Little & Ives Company, 1923.

Scheliha, Victor Ernst Von. *A Treatise on Coast Defense.* London: E & F. Spon, 1868.

Semmes, Raphael. *Memoirs of Service Afloat during the War Between the States.* New York: J. P. Kennedy & Sons, 1869.

South Carolina Convention Documents 1860-1862; Report of the Special Committee of twenty one on the communications of His Excellency Governor Pickens together with the Reports of the Heads of the Departments and other papers. Columbia: R. W. Gibbes, 1862.

Statutes at Large of the Provisional Congress of the Confederate States of America. Richmond: R. M. Smith, Printer, 1864.

The War of the Rebellion: A Compilation of the Official Records of

the Union and Confederate Armies. 130 vols. Washington, D. C.:
Government Printing Office, 1880-1901.

Thompson, R. M., and R. Wainwright, *Confidential Correspondence
of Gustavus Vasa Fox, Assistant Secretary of the Navy 1861-1865.*
2 vols., New York: Naval History Society, 1918-1919.

U. S. Bureau of the Census. *Eighth Census of the United States 1860,
Manufactures in 1860.*

U. S. Bureau of the Census. *Tenth Census of the United States: 1880,
Hall Report on the Shipbuilding Industry of the United States.*

Vandiver, Frank E., *The Civil War Diary of General Josiah Gorgas.*
University, Ala.: University of Alabama Press, 1947.

Wilson, James H. *Under the Old Flag.* 2 vols. New York: D. Appleton
& Company, 1912.

Articles

Blake, W. H. "Coal Barging in Wartime 1861-1865," *Gulf State Historical Magazine,* I (1901), 409-410.

Brooke, John Mercer. "The *Virginia* or *Merrimac*: Her Real Projector,"
Southern Historical Society Papers, XIX (1891), 3-34.

Ebaugh, David C. "David C. Ebaugh on the building of the David,"
South Carolina Historical Magazine, LIV (1955), 32-36.

Gorgas, Josiah. "Notes on the Ordnance Department of the Confederate
Government," *Southern Historical Society Papers,* XII (1884),
67-94.

"Proceedings of the Confederate Congress," *Southern Historical Society
Papers,* Vols. XLIV-LII (1923-1959).

Newspapers

Charleston *Courier.* 1862.

Columbus (Georgia) *Inquirer.* 1861-1864.

Columbus (Georgia) *Sun.* 1861-1864.

Montgomery (Alabama) *Advertiser.* 1862-1863.

New Orleans *True Delta.* 1861-1862.

Richmond *Dispatch.* 1861-1864.

Richmond *Examiner.* 1861-1865.

Richmond *Whig.* 1861-1863.

Secondary Materials

Books

Anderson, Bern. *By Sea and by River: The Naval History of the Civil War*. New York: Alfred A. Knopf, 1962.

Armes, Ethel. *The Story of Coal and Iron in Alabama*. Birmingham: Chamber of Commerce, 1910.

Barrett, John G. *The Civil War in North Carolina*. Chapel Hill: University of North Carolina Press, 1963.

Baxter, James P., III. *The Introduction of the Ironclad Warship*. Cambridge: Harvard University Press, 1933.

Bishop, J. Leander. *A History of American Manufactures from 1608 to 1860*. 3 vols. Philadelphia: Edward Young & Company, 1868.

Black, Robert C. *The Railroads of the Confederacy*. Chapel Hill: University of North Carolina Press, 1952.

Bruce, Kathleen. *Virginia Iron Manufacture in the Slave Era*. New York: The Century Company, 1931.

Canfield, Eugene B. *Notes on Naval Ordnance of the American Civil War, 1861-1865*. Washington, D. C.: The American Ordnance Association, 1960

Capers, Gerald M., Jr. *The Biography of a River Town*. Chapel Hill: University of North Carolina Press, 1939.

Castlen, Harriet. *Hope Bids Me Onward*. Savannah: Chatham Printing Company, 1945.

Cauthen, Charles C. *South Carolina Goes to War, 1860-1865*. Chapel Hill: University of North Carolina Press, 1950.

Charleston, South Carolina: The Centennial of Incorporation, 1883. Charleston: The News and Courier Book Presses, 1884.

Civil War Naval Chronology, 1861-1865. Washington, D. C.: Government Printing Office, 1961-1965.

Clark, Victor. *The History of Manufactures in the United States*. 3 vols. New York: Carnegie Institute, 1929.

Clayton, William F. *A Narrative of the Confederate States Navy*. Weldon, North Carolina: Harrell's Printing House, 1910.

Cole, Arthur C. *The Irrepressible Conflict, 1850-1865*. New York: The Macmillan Company, 1934.

Coulter, E. Merton. *The Confederate States of America, 1861-1865. A History of the South*, Vol. VII, ed. W. H. Stephenson and E. Merton Coulter. 10 vols. Baton Rouge: Louisiana State University Press, 1950.

Davis, Charles S. *Colin J. McRae: Confederate Financial Agent*. Tuscaloosa: Confederate Publishing Company, 1961.

Dew, Charles B. *Ironmaker to the Confederacy: Joseph R. Anderson and the Tredegar Iron Works.* New Haven: Yale University Press, 1966.

Dictionary of American Naval Fighting Ships. Vol. II. Washington, D. C.: Government Printing Office, 1963.

Donald, David, *Why the North Won the Civil War.* Baton Rouge: Louisiana State University Press, 1960.

Dufour, Charles L. *The Night the War Was Lost.* Garden City: Doubleday & Company, 1960.

Durkin, Joseph T. *Stephen R. Mallory: Confederate Navy Chief.* Chapel Hill: University of North Carolina Press, 1954.

Dutton, William S. *Du Pont, One Hundred and Forty Years.* New York: Charles Scribner's Sons, 1942.

Eaton, Clement. *A History of the Old South.* New York: The Macmillan Company, 1949.

——————————. *A History of the Southern Confederacy.* New York: The Macmillan Company, 1954.

Eavenson, Howard N. *The First Century and a Quarter of American Coal Industry.* Pittsburgh: Kippers Building, 1942.

Fleming, Walter L. *Civil War and Reconstruction in Alabama.* New York: Peter Smith, 1905.

Hardy, John. *Selma: Her Institutions and Her Men.* Selma, Alabama: Times Book and Job Office, 1879.

Hawk, E. Q. *Economic History of the South.* Englewood Cliffs, New Jersey: Prentice-Hall, Inc., 1934.

Hunter, Lewis, C. *Steamboats on the Western Rivers.* Cambridge: Harvard University Press, 1949.

Hutchins, John G. B. *The American Maritime Industries and Public Policy, 1789-1914* Cambridge. Harvard University Press, 1941.

Jackson, Walter M. *The Story of Selma.* Birmingham: Birmingham Printing Company, 1954.

Johns, John E. *Florida During the Civil War.* Gainesville: University of Florida Press, 1963.

Jones, Virgil C. *The Civil War At Sea.* 3 vols. New York: Holt, Rinehart, and Winston, 1960-1962.

Kendall, John S. *History of New Orleans.* 3 vols. Chicago: The Lewis Publishing Company, 1922.

Kettell, Thomas P. *Southern Wealth and Northern Profits.* New York: G. W. & J. A. Wood, 1860.

Lawrence, Alexander A. *A Present for Mr. Lincoln.* Macon, Georgia: The Ardivan Press, 1961.

Lesley, J. P. *The Iron Manufacturers Guide to Furnaces, Forges, and Rolling Mills in the United States.* New York: John Wiley, 1859.

Lonn, Ella. *Foreigners in the Confederate Army and Navy.* Chapel Hill: University of North Carolina Press, 1940.

Lytle List of Merchant Steam Vessels of the United States 1807-1868.

Mystic, Connecticut: The Steamship Historical Society of America, 1952.

Massey, Mary E. *Ersatz in the Confederacy*. Columbia: University of South Carolina Press, 1952.

Moore, Albert B. *Conscription and Conflict in the Confederacy*. New York: The Macmillan Company, 1924.

Perry, Milton F. *Infernal Machines: The Story of Confederate Submarine and Mine Warfare*. Baton Rouge: Louisiana State University Press, 1965.

Porter, John W. H. *A Record of Events in Norfolk County, Virginia*. Portsmouth, Virginia: W. A. Fisher, 1892.

Robinson, William M., Jr. *The Confederate Privateers*. New Haven: Yale University Press, 1928.

Roman, Alfred. *The Military Operations of General Beauregard in the War Between the States, 1861-1865*. 2 vols. New York: Harper & Brothers, 1884.

Scharf, J. Thomas. *History of the Confederate States Navy*. New York: Rogers & Sherwood, 1887.

Scruggs, J. H., Jr. *Alabama Steamboats, 1819-1869*. Birmingham: privately printed, 1953.

Standard, Diffie W. *Columbus, Georgia, in the Confederacy*. New York: The William-Frederick Press, 1954.

Summersell, Charles G. *The Cruise of C.S.S. Sumter*. Tuscaloosa: Confederate Publishing Company, 1965.

Thompson, Samuel B. *Confederate Purchasing Operations Abroad* Chapel Hill: University of North Carolina Press, 1935.

Todd, Herbert H. *The Building of the Confederate States Navy in Europe*. Nashville: Private edition distributed by the Joint University Libraries, 1941.

Todd, Richard C. *Confederate Finance*. Athens: University of Georgia Press, 1954.

Trexler, Harrison A. *The Confederate Ironclad Virginia (Merrimac)*. Chicago: University of Chicago Press, 1938.

Van Deusen, John G. *Economic Bases of Disunion in South Carolina*. New York: Columbia University Press, 1928.

Vandiver, Frank E. *Confederate Blockade Running Through Bermuda*. Austin: University of Texas Press, 1947.

——————— . *Ploughshares into Swords*. Austin: University of Texas Press. 1952.

——————— . *Rebel Brass: The Confederate Command System*. Baton Rouge: Louisiana State University Press, 1956.

Van Gelder, Arthur P., and Hugo Schlatter. *History of the Explosives Industry in America*. New York: Columbia University Press, 1927.

Wertenbaker, Thomas J. *Norfolk: Historic Southern Port*. Durham: Duke University Press, 1931.

Wesley, Charles H. *Negro Labor in the United States, 1850-1925.* New York: Vanguard Press, 1927.

Wiley, Bell. *Southern Negroes, 1861-1865.* New Haven: Yale University Press, 1938.

Williams, Frances L. *Matthew Fontaine Maury, Scientist of the Sea.* New Brunswick: Rutgers University Press, 1963.

Williams, T. Harry. *Beauregard: Napoleon in Gray.* Baton Rouge: Louisiana State University Press, 1954.

Woodward, Joseph H., II. *Alabama Blast Furnaces.* Woodward, Alabama: Woodward Iron Company, 1940.

Yates, Richard E. *The Confederacy and Zeb Vance.* Tuscaloosa: Confederate Publishing Company, 1958.

Yearns, Wilfred B. *The Confederate Congress.* Athens: University of Georgia Press, 1960.

Articles

Bowlby, Elizabeth. "The Role of Atlanta during the War Between the States," *Atlanta Historical Quarterly,* V (1940), 177-196.

Bradford, Sydney S. "The Negro Ironworker in Ante Bellum Virginia," *Journal of Southern History,* XXV (1959), 194-206.

Chandler, Walter. "The Memphis Navy Yard," *West Tennessee Historical Society Papers,* I (1947), 68-72.

Diamond, William. "Imports of the Confederate Government from Europe and Mexico," *Journal of Southern History,* VI (1940), 450-503.

Donnelly, Ralph W. "The Charlotte, North Carolina, Navy Yard, C.S.N." *Civil War History,* V (1959), 72-79 .

Lander, Ernest M., Jr., "Charleston: Manufacturing Center of the Old South," *Journal of Southern History,* XXVI (1960), 341.

Layton, Edwin, "Colin J. McRae and the Selma Arsenal," *Alabama Review,* XVIII (1966), 125-136.

Melvin, Philip. "Stephen Russell Mallory: Naval Statesman," *Journal of Southern History,* X (1944), 137-160.

Merrill, James M. "Confederate Shipbuilding in New Orleans," *Journal of Southern History,* XXVII (1962), 87-93.

Mitchell, Stephen S. "Atlanta the Industrial Heart of the Confederacy," *The Atlanta Historical Bulletin,* I (1930), 20-27.

Parks, William M. "Building a Warship in the Southern Confederacy," *United States Naval Institute Proceedings,* LXIX (1923), 1299-1307.

Ramsdell, Charles W. "The Control of Manufacturing by the Confederate Government," *Mississippi Valley Historical Review,* VIII (1921), 231-249.

Stavisky, Leonard P. "Industrialism in Ante Bellum Charleston," *Journal of Negro History,* XXXVI (1951), 302-322.

Stephen, Walter W. "The Brooke Guns from Selma," *Alabama Historical Quarterly*, XX (1958), 462-475.

Still, William N., Jr. "Confederate Shipbuilding in Mississippi," *Journal of Mississippi History*, XXX (1968), 291-303.

————. "Selma and the Confederate States Navy," *Alabama Review*, XIV (1962), 19-37.

————. "Confederate Naval Strategy: The Ironclad," *Journal of Southern History* XXVII (1961), 330-343.

————. "Confederate Naval Policy and the Ironclad," *Civil War History*, IX (1963), 145-156.

————. "Facilities for the Construction of War Vessels in the Confederacy," *Journal of Southern History*, XXXI (1965), 285-304.

————. "The Career of the Confederate Ironclad *Neuse*," North *Carolina Historical Review*, XLIII (1966), 1-13.

————. "The Confederate Ironclad *Missouri*," *Louisiana Studies*, IV (1965), 101-110.

Townsend, Leah. "The Confederate Gunboat *Peedee*," *South Carolina Historical Magazine*, LX (1959), 66-73.

Trexler, Harrison A. "The Confederate Navy Department and the Fall of New Orleans," *Southwest Review*, XIX (1933), 88-102.

Vandiver, Frank E. "The Shelby Iron Works in the Civil War; A Study of Confederate Industry," *Alabama Review*, I (1948), 12-26, 111-127, 203-217.

Dissertations and Theses

Brooke, George M., Jr. "John Mercer Brooke," 2 vols. Diss., University of North Carolina, 1955.

Jackson, Joyce. "History of the Shelby Iron Company, 1862-1868." Master's thesis, University of Alabama, 1948.

Neill, John H., Jr. "Shipbuilding in Confederate New Orleans." Master's thesis, Tulane University, 1940.

Wells, Tom H., "The Confederate Navy: A Study in Organization." Diss., Emory University, 1963.

Index